I0141514

(We Live on)

The Same Road

A NOVEL OF LEARNING AND PERSEVERANCE

By

Keith Parfitt

For Chester L. Parfitt and Harold “Skeets” Wickham. One helped to defeat a fascist regime that felt euthanasia was the definitive answer to those of us less than perfect. The other employed those of us less than perfect along-side him long before it was the popular thing to do.

Keith Neil Parfitt
United States of America Copyright Office
Maureen Publishing
ISBN# 978-0-9797169-9-7

 Published in U.S.A. 2007. For bulk or discount orders contact maureenpublishing.com online or snail mail at
Maureen Publishing
1 Erie Ave. Cuddebackville N.Y. 12729

Contents **2**

INTRODUCTION **3**

One
Welcome to the neighborhood **4**

Two
Ferris House **13**

Three
Earn your keep **23**

Four
The weekend visitor **44**

Five
The next step **63**

Six
Fun in the community **75**

Seven
Free at Last **104**

Eight
Welcome Back **114**

Nine
Justice for all **129**

Ten
Inversion **164**

Epilogue
168

Introduction

When I began writing this story I had just started working among people with disabilities after a six-year hiatus from the human services field.

The epidemic of autism was foremost in my mind. I have worked with autistic individuals as well as others with various afflictions. For some years while I was employed in community residences I assisted people with the same chores that we all deal with on a daily basis. I observed and experienced the frustrations which arise when simple needs and wants cannot be conveyed in an ordinary fashion.

Although I did not create this story to address specifically the controversy on the cause or causes of Autism or any other hardship termed developmental disability, I feel that all potential sources must be explored. Given that it is inhumane to inflict suffering where it can be avoided, 'private entities' that are found culpable must pay the price no matter what the cost. Those affected will continue to pay dearly.

The purpose of this tale is to show how those of us who are less fortunate often labor under a heavier yoke than the rest. I also hope to draw attention to those suffering with life-changing ailments with the intention that they will ultimately have the ability in our society to attempt success as the rest of us do.

As I wrote this fictional account, I hoped that all who read this will keep one thing in mind: although we are all very diverse, we all have the same needs, wants, and desires. When someone is trapped within themselves it is the duty, indeed the responsibility, of the rest of us to assist, explore, and prevent this from happening wherever we are able.

We truly are more alike than we are different.

1
WELCOME TO THE NEIGHBORHOOD

IT was a road like any other in rural northeastern USA. The light blue van drove casually down this particular road on a sunny afternoon in May, as if it were a leaf floating in a brook. If you were a passenger in that van peering out the window, you would have seen the new leaves of spring trees, the early flowering of daffodils and crocuses, along with the vibrant wet green of people's lawns lining the sides of the road.

You would also have seen older houses with wood shiplap siding or asbestos shingle closer to the road and to each other. This was how houses were erected in that period after WW-II when a flurry of housing construction attempted to accommodate our troops returning home from war and the ensuing prosperity.

As you continued on your journey, you would also see some recently constructed homes covered with enough vinyl to start a record company in the 1950s; 'McMansions' some had nicknamed them.

Most of these newer constructs included more expansive lawns and were set back a greater distance from the road and from each other. You would also notice that of these houses, a few had very wide side yards with ample trees and shrubs as a buffer between them and their neighbors. This gave them the illusion of privacy much greater than reality. Other houses, again the more dated ones, would be as close on their side yards as to make one think of the proverbial trailer park atmosphere of much less extravagant accommodations, but still somewhat removed from tenement living. This was precisely what a lean Asian man named Hector Chang saw as he sat in the far back seat of the van. He accompanied by several other people also gazing through the windows in what seemed sheer wonder or total indifference.

How this affected Hector we cannot know as we are 'regular'. The label 'regular' was sometimes used by people with disabilities to refer to people that do not have disabilities. If one was not afflicted with a disability, then one would be a regular person or without obvious flaw or affliction.

Hector looked about 26 years old, because of his youthful face and otherwise waif-like appearance, but he was actually 41. He was tall, about six feet six inches. He was so lean one would think at first glance that he was emaciated. This of course was not the case; Hector was so active that he simply burned calories at an outlandish rate as compared to most regular people, and alleged non-regular people for that matter.

Hector's face was pressed squarely against the passenger side window, thinking thoughts that only God, the devil, and he knew as he watched the scenery pass. Hector pulled back from the window and began to rock back and forth gently as was his fancy much of the time, apparently finished with his observations.

If we followed the direction of his previous gaze we would notice that most houses on the ten-and-a-half-mile road were neatly kept, if not expansively landscaped. Some may wonder if Hector noticed this fact. Others don't care what he may have noticed. It all depended on what kind of person was observing Hector in the first place. Not all people in a neighborhood were considerate of others, especially if those being considered were 'retarded' people, much less the already indigenous neighbors who were purportedly regular people.

The neighbors, about whom Hector could not possibly yet know, were a mixture of commuters who held employment in N.Y. City: cops, firefighters, various levels of corporate middle management, and a few upper level professionals living side-by-side with local people, people whose families had lived in the area for generations. People whose ancestors had owned farms or worked on local farms which no longer brought the products into being that they had in their heyday. The few that survived were trimmed down to virtual hobby farms. They had fields stretching back far enough into the distance behind the dwellings to give a good flavor of country living or were vacant land that was simply left for nature to reclaim.

Some of the people on Ferris Road socialized with each other on a regular basis and some kept to themselves. As with any regular American town. Soccer moms took their children to after school events while others allowed television, the ever ready companion and steadfast babysitter, as well as the even newer substitute, computers, do their parenting for them. Still others did those shadowy things people do when they get home from work or shopping or whatever it is they did during their daily routine which helped them find solace, or purpose, or pleasure in their limited existence.

These neighbors didn't have block parties as grid-development neighborhoods might, and were not nearly as familiar as people become on 'the block' in big-city neighborhoods. They certainly were not as intimate as in times long past when one neighbor's troubles were considered everyone's troubles. But as human nature went, there was one thing that could always be relied upon: the ever-present curse, or pastime, or distraction, of good old fashioned chit-chat, idle talk, or the more accusatory stimulating moniker: Gossip!

That wondrous miracle of communication which survived thousands of years of history, giving rise to so many of humankind's woes throughout times past. Known for its reliability of speed if not the accuracy of its content, or consideration of personal reputation.

This bane of society was in full swing in the autumn of 1997. Little known to Hector and his fellow travelers, this phenomenon from throughout the ages was to begin a set of events of consequence which would bring a small town to the proverbial brink. Well, if not the town, then some fascinating players in the ongoing drama of this town.

As the van pulled into a long driveway, Hector could not possibly have known the tumultuous set of occurrences that had converged to get him and his companions to this point, at this house. Or worse yet, what would be in store for them in the immediate and unforeseeable future.

The central focus and source of this earth-shattering information, gossip, came from the local town hall, particularly the town clerk (what a surprise). It seemed Linda, the town clerk, a dyed-black-haired-red-lipsticked-saggy-jowled harpy of a woman had informed her favorite chit-chat partner that there were some undesirables attempting to move into the peaceful area of Ferris Road, and by performing this act of arrogant intrusion, disrupt the tranquility of the neighborhood as well as the overall welfare of the town.

These new interlopers were even worse than the soy- and -grass-eating Buddhists had been when they started to invade some years back. Linda told Chit-Chat (as some of the other town regulars labeled Linda's gossip buddy), that this new threat to the harmony of the community was not the usual run-of-the-mill non-Christian religion. A totally alien culture who did not eat meat (which, by the way, the community had adjusted to quite well). But that was not the point. It was much worse; it was a known and ancient blight, one that everyone had encountered at some time in their life, and well feared by many modern communities. "A seditious bane on any civilization or even un-civilization" Linda stated. Like some of those heathenish ones overseas. But certainly it did not belong in their town or on Ferris Road.

"That's right, Mrs. Chat," Linda admonished. "It 's one of those retard houses."

To say that this was offensive to some in the community was a gross understatement. This was nothing less than an undermining of the affronted individuals' civil rights and personal freedoms. According to some of the more aggressive elements in the opposition, it was nothing less than a shredding of the very fabric of American society. It was time for the good citizens to stand up and fight: to cleanse this curse, a call to arms as it were. Time to have neighborhood meetings, pass around petitions, call your state senators, and raise a general ruckus. But try as they might (and after pounding the pavement, burning the phone lines, and maybe spending $20.00 on postage), on one cool evening in the autumn of 1997, a town hall meeting convened at 7:00 P.M. with all the usual suspects in attendance. As Supervisor Samuel Norvaski, a large man with a full head of bushy white hair and a sturdy frame beginning to go to pot, officially called the meeting to order. He knew he would rather be somewhere else.

Many homeowners devised and presented numerous and well-thought out 'legitimate' reasons to block the impending calamity.

"Our property values will drop," was the contention of Harriet Edmondson, a hawkish salt-and-peppered olive-skinned woman.

"Our tax rate will rise, because those people don't pay taxes, you know," Mr. Edmondson chimed in, slyly pleased with his insightfulness as he scratched his perpetually bulbous red W.C. Fields nose acquired from too much alcohol.

"Please, one at a time, state your concerns and they will be answered in turn," Supervisor Norvaski said with a counterfeit air of concern. A very smelly overweight man with a handlebar moustache and a shaven tattooed head raised his hand to be recognized. Supervisor Norvaski pointed his gavel at the man.

"Please stand and state your name sir."

The man stood up with an attitude of rabid expostulation.

"My name is Jay Klupkick, and I want you to know you bring a dangerous element into the neighborhood; those people with their super-retard-strength will hurt our children!"

"You extraordinary oaf," Miss Schneling exclaimed, a local grammar school teacher with a mousy brown haired appearance and a weak quivering chin. "How ignorant can one person possibly be?" she asked no one in particular. "You don't even have children!!!"

Klupkick viciously cut her off with a slice of his fat hand as he rounded on her, pinning her with his barely concealed savage look.

"Those people with their hypersexual drive will rape our daughters or worse yet our sons. They ain't right, ya know. They look funny, they smell funny, and they act funny." He ticked these points off on his beefy fingers, and as the profound words of wisdom expounded from Klupkick, spittle started to appear at the side of his mouth as if he was relishing a tasty steak and onion dinner. As Klupkick finished his points he turned back to the supervisor with what, for him, was a theatrical flourish.

Other good citizens on both sides of the altercation joined in to exercise their right of free speech.

"They walk funny."

"They talk funny."

"They dress funny."

"They're dirty."

"They scare the children."

"They scare the elderly."

"They pick their nose."

"They pick their ears."

"They pick their ass."

Likewise, the defenders courageously and vehemently let their emotions take full rein.

"You pick your ass, too, for God's sake; you urinate in your yard." An out of control Miss Schneling contended almost hysterically—finally getting up the nerve to glare back at Klupkick.

"For God sakes, they're like children," Joan Ferris interrupted with an emotional passion welling up in her usually calm demeanor.

Klupkick rounded on her.

"It was your brother-in-law that sold those retards that house in the first place," shouted Klupkick to Joan Ferris, aiming his dark vitriol at her, trying to intimidate her like any common whore, since he considers all of the fairer sex to be in the same category.

Joan shot a look of blue fire from her usually kind bright blue eyes. Like a laser beam it struck at the contorted pig face of Klupkick (or, as some called him, fat belly Jay). Klupkick almost flinched openly, as strong women both frightened and enraged him simultaneously. But never being one to back away from a fight, especially with someone he perceived to be weaker, he fired a look of black venom right back at her.

As the two locked eyes in a silent battle of wills, the rest of the assemblage continued to escalate the impassioned discussion with vigor.

"They're innocent souls, for goodness sakes," interjected a senior named Marina Beastly, a local spinster, lonely as the day was long.

"They're not innocent," Mr. Edmondson interrupted. "They do perverted things in them institutions they come from. I heard about it from my brother's cousin's sister who used to work in the state hospital across the river."

Supervisor Norvaski looked on in growing trepidation, wondering how things had gotten so out of control so quickly.

"Shit," slipped out under his breath as he reached over and started to bang the gavel. *"I ain't going to let this turn into another long damn night; I have to end this quick, Momma's waiting at home with dinner,"* he thought to himself. ***"ORDER! ORDER!"*** he continued to bang the gavel. The sharp sound of the hardwood gavel on the striker plate eventually restored a grumbling silence to the hall.

Klupkick was the first to break the stare with Joan, angry for letting a damn split-tail (another malicious slur he used to refer to all females) back him down.

Norvaski addressed the good people of the community with his best bureaucratic intonation.

“This meeting’s only purpose tonight was to gather some opinions and information from the community on the efforts of Disabled People of America Inc.'s possible use of the property at 350 Ferris Road as a community residence for disabled adults. In other words,” he intoned ominously. “A home for the retarded. I'd say I have about all the opinions I need for tonight. The town thanks all of you for attending. Any further opinions on this matter will be accepted in writing by the town clerk during normal business hours. This meeting is adjourned”

The gavel hit its mark like a gun shot. The gathered assembly let go with low key grumbling protest, and some more boisterous comments also emitted from the good townspeople who were more fervently opposed.

The town officials, including Peter Anderson, the Chief of Police, Supervisor Norvaski, and the town lawyer, Barrister Harold Smithson, left the podium for the relative safety of a private office.

In his office Norvaski turned to Smithson with an inquiring look furrowing his already wrinkled forehead. Smithson looked back trying to read Norvaski's mind. These men had known each other since they were in grammar school and he did not find this difficult to accomplish.

“There is not a lot we can do to stop something like this and we shouldn't try,” began the lawyer. “They’re pretty commonplace these days, what with the budget cuts at the state level and the events of the last thirty-plus years concerning the disability laws. It turns out that these community residences are a lot cheaper to run," Smithson emphasized, finishing his thought.

He was a slight, bald man with piercing dark eyes whose gaze affirmed what he asserted to Norvaski with a candid look.

Norvaski looked down at his hands on the desk.

“I got nothing against the retarded people. They have as much rights as the rest of us and most people feel the same way,” Norvaski acknowledged.

“There weren't a lot of people at this meeting and those that don't like it will get used to the idea, just like they did the Buddhists,” Smithson pondered to no one in particular.

Peter Anderson, Chief of Police, addressed both men for the first time. “Those ones you’re talkin' about still call the station every Sunday when the Buddhist bell goes off to complain it's against the noise ordinances, and those venerable neighbors have been here 10 years now. So I won't put money on that.”

The other two men gazed at him, dejected that he wouldn’t let them have this fantasy, if only for a short while. Norvaski broke the brief enchantment.

"Well gentleman, the die is cast, as the saying goes. I'm goin' home to see about my dinner before my wife tries to banish me," Norvaski muttered with some finality.

"Me too," Smithson agreed.

Chief Anderson concurred and the three men left to go into the parking lot.

As they said their goodnights, it seemed as though the air was cooler than it should be for this time of year. They all departed and soon forgot about the newest event to hit the small hamlet, at least for a little while. All three had about as much of an idea of what was coming as Hector Chang did.

Further efforts by a select few of the good citizens of the community to block the invasion of the new neighbors at 350 Ferris Road were in vain, no matter what apparently very good reasons were given in defense of their noble stance. Come the spring 1998, the house with the address known as 350 Ferris Road was destined to be known by some in the neighborhood as *that retard house.*

Fortunately, not all felt that way and many others were too concerned with living their own lives to worry about the house or what might transpire there. Consequently, little thought was put into the matter by most of the surrounding neighbors. As a matter of a fact, of the dozen or so that actually showed up at the town meeting to state their concerns on the issue, only about half were opposed. And of those, only one of them lived in close vicinity to the house, say within a mile. Of the others in the neighborhood, some of course knew disabled people they worked with, or had relatives in their families who were disabled, or had been in contact with the less-able fleetingly throughout their lives.

These neighbors had absolutely no animosity toward the new additions at 350 Ferris Road.

This attitude was even worse to the locals, as they thought of themselves (even though some of them have only lived in the neighborhood for at best five years), who were in opposition. Now at least they knew who the traitors were.

One night in a local smoky bar named The Hazard Inn, 'they' vowed among themselves to fight until the interlopers were driven out, never to return, and to teach their bleeding-heart neighbors a lesson they would never forget. Of course 'they' were Jay Klupkick and his faithful follower, and only friend, an individual that did any odd job he could find simply to make some drinking money—Seymour Hinkel.

"We should make it a living hell for those retards," Klupkick grumbled over his domestic beer. "Did you see those mixed breeds staggering around up there like some sort of spazzes?" he inquired of Seymour, the only person left in town who still listened to him.

Seymour, not being renowned for his cognitive abilities, came back with a brilliant riposte.

"What ere you going to do Jay?" he slurred, as he looked into his beer bottle as though there were something enthralling inside, something that might reveal a long time unknown mystery of the ages.

"I don't know what I'll do, but if it weren't for those Ferris', those bastards that ride the tard-cart wouldn't even be here. It's 'cause that split-tail wife of that Marc Ferris and Ferris himself that helped get them in that house, somethin' will happen; those people always cause trouble. I won't have to do anything and the town's people will see when one of their daughters gets raped, you'll see then, they'll run them out of town themselves."

Seymour simply downed the rest of his beer and let out a feeble belch.

Naturally, those with little compassion for the less than fortunate also have just as little drive to stick with their ill made promises. By the time all the dust settled a few months later, there were only a few stalwart sore losers still grumbling about the new neighbors at 350 Ferris Road. But alas, there was always time for these people later, as there was never a shortage of them…

2
Ferris House
(Home Sweet Home)

The house had belonged to John Ferris. He was a true local, as his family was one who actually owned a farm in the area for more generations than the town had been incorporated. He had received an exorbitant amount of money from Disabled People of America, Inc. for an old farmhouse with six bedrooms and enough space left over to accommodate the staff that came along with the new residents.

Even now, John Ferris still owned a vast amount of land. Along with the rest of what was left of a large farm family, currently consisting of a sister and several cousins, the Ferris family commanded respect and were known by others in the local area as fair dealers. Fortunately, the neighbor to one side of 350 Ferris Road was his cousin Marc Ferris, husband to Joan, who had spoken up after a positive fashion at the meeting the fall before. Much of the rest of the Ferris family had moved on to other areas as they had profited greatly from the real-estate boom of the mid-90s. Only Marc and Joan Ferris were left on that end of Ferris Road, 348 Ferris Lane to be exact, right smack- dab next door to the newest additions to the neighborhood.

By the end of May, while nature was in full swing with green everywhere, shortly after he and his companions had moved in, Hector peered at the new neighbors' house from behind some forsythia bushes in the backyard of his new home, gently rocking back and forth as was his habit. As he rocked to and fro gently and spied on his new neighbors he saw one of those houses with a large front yard and a remarkably well kept rose garden. All this adjacent to his little hide-a-way. If he were to turn and look back over his shoulder at his new residence, he would see a lawn over 180 feet in length stretching from the road to his house. He would also see a driveway about 200 feet in length. To the side of the house the driveway ended in a small blacktop parking lot with a van and a car on one side, two or three cars on the other side with no painted line parking spaces, and a large dumpster.

The side yards were generous, with lots of covering and screening foliage. The grounds were well kept and the house had been sided with new white vinyl siding over the old wood shiplap siding. Although the Ferris' had no problem with their new neighbors, they did miss having family live next door as many would. But certainly Hector did not know this. He really had no perspective to speak of in this way as he had developed his viewpoint in an institution.

"Hector," sounded a call from inside his new home. "S-S-Sam said for you to h-help me set the table for lunch." Chico, an Hispanic man with the customary short stature and facial distinctiveness common to someone with Downs Syndrome, emerged from the back door to summon Hector.

Chico liked Hector and considered him his best new friend, although he had actually lived with Hector at the house for only a short period of time. Chico had very few close friends in his plus years. The experience of having a best buddy was enjoyable for him to say the least.

At the sound of his name Hector froze for an instant, like a cheetah stalking its prey—he stood still as a stone, watching the neighbors' house—then he began to rock gently back and forth once more. Chico came up behind Hector and touched him gently on his arm; Hector, in a sudden burst of energy, like a gazelle fleeing for its life, sprinted past Chico to the back door of their new house and disappeared inside. Chico shook his head with a little smile on his face, a mannerism he acquired over the years watching those who had worked with him while he lived in institutions, not knowing why they were doing it at the time, but understanding now. Then casually he followed his friend inside.

Less than 30 days passed. It was now early in June 1998 with the clean, flowery fragrance of late spring in the air, in preparation for a glorious summer and the absolute beauty of multi-colored diverse flora adorning the world. If one were to walk down the driveway of 350 Ferris Road (or maybe were a nearby neighbor) one would notice a sound coming from the House a high keening noise. The sound was so steady in pitch and constant in duration that at first they might think it was some type of gardening machinery commonly used in a neighborhood where people were doing spring maintenance and cleaning in their yards. They would be clearing brush from the previous winter, as well as the lavish growth of a new season.

As you advanced toward the house, a faint but audible slapping/thumping noise would also become evident that would of course confuse the idle eavesdropper. The keening noise would begin to transform. Inside, if you were a fly on the wall, you would see the source of this commotion.

Hector was sitting on a couch, rocking fiercely back and forth, slapping his chest with his right hand as he slammed his body against the back of the couch with each backward movement. The leanness that this aerobic activity imparted to Hector made him the envy of some around him since he could (and did) eat like a horse and never gained weight. He was essentially two percent body fat.

Hector was in the throes of recall. And he possessed a recollection better than one might imagine. He was purportedly of sub-standard intelligence to those around him. But Hector was autistic, and instead enjoyed an innate intelligence that few, if any, were becoming aware of. Especially those inside the great research halls of academia. Unlike many of us, he could remember back to when he was two or three years old. Of course he didn't realize he was two or three years old at the time, as he was coming into conscious self-awareness, much like many people were at that time in their development. But Hector did not do what most people did after having moved on, after growing older. He did not relegate the past experiences to some dusty lock box in his psyche, never to be brought back to conscious thought.

Some say that's what separated us from the animals, self-awareness—naturally, others felt differently, as they considered people merely the human animal.

Many, in those early days, looked at Hector and others similar to him as if they were no better than animals. And like animals it was felt they had to be controlled and confined so they would not foul society. As these damaged individuals truly had no purpose, these same great minds generously had the humanity not to destroy these poor unfortunates out of hand, which had been accepted practice of other societies in what one hoped were bygone days. So as an alternative, they compassionately would warehouse them in institutions. This kept society safe and normal.

Hector's parents knew that something was different with their son: he did not do all those things normal babies do as they develop. He did not smile or laugh. He did not begin to speak as was common development for a child of his age. He seemed distant from human contact.

Back in 1962, after taking Hector to the appropriate physicians, these same expert doctors told them that there was no hope for their son: that nothing could be done to make him normal, that the best thing they could do was put him in a state institution where he could be properly cared for and to forget they had ever had this child. This, the experts said, is what was best for them and for society at large.

Being first generation Korean immigrants, coupled with the shame of having a retarded—tainted son, they complied with the expert's advice. With great sorrow and agonizing trepidation, Mr. and Mrs. Chang committed Hector to an institution on Staten Island as a ward of the state.

The day the men in the white coats came to collect him, to take him to the Willowbrook State School for the developmentally disabled (of Geraldo fame), Hector was very frightened. He felt something in the air, so to speak, and he had not met these men prior to that day. Previously, anytime he left the house, his mother had always gone with him and there was a routine to which he had become accustomed. But this was different; his Mom had his coat ready as usual, but not hers. As Mr. and Mrs. Chang let the men into their small house, Hector instinctively knew the jig was up. His parents miserably gave Hector over to the men and naturally emotions ran very high for all concerned, even the men in the white coats.

Hector, being very insightful to all events around him, became a repudiation of the affair taking place, and would not proceed to the door as requested. This disturbed everyone even further, and the men endeavored to escort Hector out of the house with as little fuss as possible, as this was their job. After all, they were professionals. Needless to say, Hector began to act out by hitting himself in the head, screaming, and jumping up and down (as many of us regular people might also have done in a similar situation—or at least we would have liked to). This behavior, of course, was unallowable by the men. They had no other choice but to act courageously and physically subdue Hector so he did not harm himself or those around him. This, after all, was their job, and they did it well.

The trauma was so intense for Mr. and Mrs. Chang that they were unable to forgive themselves and did not contact Hector after the event. The tremendous guilt that ensued would follow them to the grave. But this did nothing to address Hector's suffering.

This was only one of the troubling memories that haunted Hector incessantly. It presented him with a feeling of loss and emotional agony which would of course torture anyone. Although he didn't deliberately drag this intense ache to the forefront of his understanding. Nevertheless, 36 years later, as he was sitting on the couch next to a wall, rocking back and forth violently and making disparaging keening sounds. He slapped his head with both hands. This was only one of an assortment of specters which plagued Hector Chang through wake and sleep, day and night, all his life.

As Hector went through his usual episode, a man about 5' 8" with a lean wiry build and close cropped blond hair calmly stepped into the doorway.

"Hector, can I help you with something?" the man asked.

As the man unobtrusively approached, Hector's actions became more frantic. The man gently sidled up beside Hector where he rocked on the couch and lightly touched Hector's shoulder with his hand. Hector leapt to his feet, pivoted quickly, and faced the man. He grabbed the man by his shoulders. The man, whose name was Elmer, gently put his hands on top of Hector's wrist's. Hector pushed tensely on Elmer's shoulders, trying to push away the primordial memories of terror that only a child could experience—memories that intruded on his too active mind like a specter returned from a dark grave. Elmer spoke gently to Hector and moved with him while he experienced the painful throes of his memory. Shortly Hector began to calm down. His frantic movements slowed—his muscles began to grow weary and fatigued. After several minutes Hector was past this current crisis. His mind came into focus, into the present; he saw Elmer instead of the white coated men from so long ago.

"Come on Hector, it's time for breakfast," Elmer suggested, maintaining his calm demeanor.

Hector rose from the tortured place in his mind and accompanied Elmer into the dining room with five other people just starting breakfast. They were seated around an oak polyurethaned dining room table cluttered with boxes of dry cereal, several half gallon cartons of low fat milk, and a few pitchers of orange juice.

Nancy Boorsman, a burly young woman with short brown hair and soft brown eyes over a pixie nose and chin, looked up from the table as Hector and Elmer entered.

"Hi Hector. Are you ready for breakfast?" she asked in a friendly manner.

Hector hurried to his chair and automatically grabbed a box of Honey Nut Cheerios sitting on the table, dumped them into his bowl. He then haphazardly splashed milk onto the cereal from a half gallon carton within easy reach. He began to eat, and in some sense, relief inundated throughout his stressed frame. He endeavored to fill a void that could not truly be satiated by food alone. As Hector ate, facing down toward his bowl of cereal, his eyes automatically looked around the table, watching everyone else as they ate. This was his habit, actually a defensive coping skill developed over years of institutional living.

Ike, one of the people at the table, stared at Hector and started a slow giggling. Ike did nothing faster than flowing molasses due to his impeded brain function. Chico glanced at Hector to make sure he was alright.

Elmer looked at Nancy Boorsman.

"Did you read the new addition to the short-term treatment plan for Abigail?" he asked.

Abigail, another individual eating breakfast at the table, briefly flicked her eyes up from her food, then back down. She started a strange sing-song abstract melody intoned in response to seemingly nothing in particular. Nancy gave Elmer an 'are you stupid look'.

"I helped Abigail put them in there, right Abigail?"

Nancy offered in Abigail's direction making it a point to include her in the conversation. Abigail seemingly ignored her and continued to eat, but the nonsensical tune shortly abated. The others at the table ate their breakfast in what passed for a routine manner in the surroundings.

Nancy looked at Elmer again, "We'll talk about it after everyone gets off to work and program."

As they finished breakfast and were in turn shooed away from the table, Chico, Hector, Ike, Clark, and Elmer end up in the upstairs bathroom. Nancy, Abigail, and Sally went to the downstairs bathroom. For a while we heard loud discussion from the ladies bathroom as Nancy and Sally went back and forth over face washing.

"But my face is clean," Sally whined.

"If it were, I wouldn't ask you to wash it . . . just look in the mirror," Nancy coaxed. Sally finally looked into the mirror and saw some grape jelly.

"Oh," escaped her lips. Then she got a wash cloth and went to work.

In the upstairs bathroom Chico was the last one brushing his teeth. The others had finished, and were either in the TV room or just hanging out waiting for the next step in their routine. Hector was gently rocking back and forth looking at nothing in particular, and Ike was peering intently out the window as if he were a WWII spotter searching for enemy aircraft. As Ike waited to announce the van's arrival, Clark nervously watched TV, and his intent look migrated from Ike at the window to the TV and back again. Elmer was downstairs with everyone else waiting for Chico. He went to the bottom of the steps.

"Chico," he shouted up the steps. "Hurry up; the van will be here soon."

"Ok Elmer, I'm almost done," came from upstairs.

Chico looked at himself in the mirror opened his eyes wider, and then opened his mouth. He made a funny face and then smiled. Chico was a 43-year-old man with Down- Syndrome. As he looked into the mirror, he knew that he looked different from other people, but this never bothered him much. Most people at the agency treated him no differently than anyone else. Most of them figure that maybe someone like Chico had it hard enough, so why alienate him further.

Born in Brooklyn of Hispanic parents in the 1950s, it was of course not known that Chico would be born as a 'Mongoloid' which was the popularterm at the time. This event caused considerable difficulty in the family with five other normal brothers and sisters. With money from Chico's dad's two jobs in short supply, things were even harder for his family.

Louis, the eldest boy in the family, was ashamed of his sibling on a deep level. Being in a good Catholic family and sometimes stuck in outdated modes of thinking, the guilt and shame for his family's image was profound. But he still protected his little brother when the neighborhood boys tried to make sport of Chico.

Some of his other brothers and sisters were not as upset but still had the same gnawing guilt of not having a completely normal family. It was always lurking below the surface; always a sore spot eating away at their family's perceived dignity. Chico, no matter what the apparent concern, did not worry, as he had a ready friendliness about himself that could be infectious.

Maria, the oldest child in the family, would not let guilt take over her thinking, and was able to love him unrestrainedly. She took him wherever she could, and it was this early experience of love from his sister that would give him strength and patience with those he encountered throughout his life.

As Chico had been contemplating some of these thoughts, he heard Ike's proclamation.

"The van's here," Ike bellowed over his shoulder as he walked out the door swinging his lunch-box back and forth as a child might.

"Chico, it's the bus, you've been brushing your teeth for ten minutes, I'm sure they're clean now." Elmer was looking upstairs from the bottom of the steps with a 'hurry up' look on his face. They heard a 'honk' from the driveway.

Ike piped up from outside the back door. "Come on Chico, the bus."

Chico came back from his childhood memories then he quickly wiped the toothpaste from his face and headed down to the kitchen.

Elmer was handing plastic lunch box coolers out to Chico, Hector, and Clark. "Bye guys, I'll see you this afternoon," he murmured.

Chico smiled and looked Elmer directly in the eye. "G-good-bye Elmer, s-see you later."

"Wait a minute," Elmer uttered. He grabbed a paper-towel from the rack and wiped some errant toothpaste from the side of Chico's mouth.

Chico smiled at Elmer appreciatively as he headed out toward the van with Hector automatically following him. Ike turned and gave Elmer 'the finger,' then hurried to get on the van and find his seat. He no longer looked in Elmer's direction, as if this very act kept him shielded.

Clark led up the rear automatically telling Ike, "you're not supposed to give Elmer the finger. Elmer, he's giving you the finger again."

"Thanks for telling me, Clark," Elmer answered calmly.

Clark passed through the door and onto the van. It rolled down the driveway, and disappeared into the distance.

Elmer walked back into the house. As he walked through the door, Nancy told Abigail and Sally to go out to the car; she'd be there in half a minute. The women obediently complied.

"Did Ike give you the finger again?" she asked, as she gave Elmer a wily grin.

"Yeah, but that's only because we did a really good job on his teeth today. Sure he was upset, but you know it had to be done. I've told him again and again you gotta' brush your teeth every 24 hours. I think he is always going to revolt and good for him. We only have to teach him a more appropriate way of expressing himself."

"Why should you make him do something you don't do?" Nancy told Elmer as she headed for the door.

Elmer gave her the finger. Nancy laughed as she casually proceeded through the door to take Abigail and Sally to work.

Elmer continued into the office, a room off the dining room, sat down at the desk and logged onto the computer. He instant messaged Shau-Shing, a house manager at 3 Shawnee Drive, another agency house in an adjoining town.

"So how's the project?" Elmer tapped the enter key.

At the Shawnee House sat a Taiwanese man, also typing on a keyboard.

"In three months every house in the agency will be linked; anyone that wants to, can instant-message anyone else in the agency." *Enter.*

"That's very exciting," Elmer mumbled to himself as he typed. "Ike likes to talk to that guy Bartholomew in the house on Rover Drive when he's enthusiastic." *Enter.*

"I know what you mean," Shau-Shing typed back, "Sherry likes to talk to that guy Mr. Dean in the house in Fallsburg." *Enter.*

"They're getting more and more like normal people everyday," Elmer typed. *Enter.*

"Too bad for them, huh?" Shau-Shing typed back. *Enter.*

"Yeah I know," Elmer typed. "Who'd have thought that people who lived in institutions for 20 years and more would have had the dream to be like us? Once they learn what we're like, they might want to go back to being sheltered." *Enter.*

"Don't give me more of your twisted philosophy," Shau-Shing typed back to Elmer. "I have to go do my shift notes, it's almost quittin' time." *Enter.*

Shau-Shing logged off, Elmer sat in front of the office computer for a moment, gazed at the wall, and listened to the sound of the spring birds. Then he pulled out a green binder and started doing his progress notes for the month.

"*It seems like I'm always behind in my paper work,*" Elmer thought to himself…

3
Earn Your Keep (Another Day in the Salt Mines)

Hector felt as though he were floating eight feet off the floor. He knew he was sitting at the table along with everyone else in his work group, but it seemed as though he were looking down at 20 people in a large room all sitting at long tables. This was a visual perception he sometimes experienced in this setting. There were three regulars, as Hector thought of them, walking around the room assisting a variety of people with different disabilities, in various states of interest. It had always been like this for Hector. Occasionally, it depended on the setting; sometimes not.

The industrial refrigerator kicked on across the room with with a horrendous bone-level, ruthless abrasive sound and no one reacted. They just went on with what they were doing.

"How could they not notice this," Hector frantically wondered? To Hector the sound cut through him with the agony of a hot poker being rammed into his ears . . . the fluorescent lights were constantly flickering at a rate of 60 flickers per second. This also was perceived by Hector, and it caused even more anguish. (Think of how some people were with strobe lights)—Hector cannot filter this out.

On one side, Hector had a little plastic bin of combs, on the other side a little plastic bin of plastic envelopes. As some others were doing in the room, he was to take a comb, insert it in an envelope and put it in a third bin in front of him. He knew he was expected to put a certain amount of combs from the bin into the plastic envelopes … flicker … flicker … flicker … and into the third bin. Hector picked up a comb from the bin and tried to put it into the little plastic envelope, but the stiff plastic envelope did not open easily—his hand began to tense up and shake a little—the medication they gave him at the house sedated him, making him sluggish—clumsier than he would have otherwise been—bang—rrrrrrrrrrrr the industrial refrigerator kicked on again.

*"**Can't filter it out!!!**"* Hector thought frantically. Rrrrrrrrrrrrrr ... flicker ... flicker ... flicker ... rrrrrrrrrrrrrr ... someone coughed across the room—someone was mumbling to themselves. This all was adding to Hector's overload. Mumble … mumble ... rrrrrrrrrrrrrr ... flicker ... flickerrrrrrrrrrr. Cough ... mumble … rrrrrrrrrrrrrrr. As some others were doing in the room, Hector bravely still tried to take a comb—insert it into an envelope— and put it in the third bin in front of him. He became even more ham-fisted in his attempts.

"Damn-it," he thought, *"Can't get the damned comb in the damned envelope."*

Hector dropped the comb and the envelope and began to rock back and forth … tapping his chest with his right hand; this provided him a minuscule outlet for the gathering tension.

Fred, one of the regulars, came over to Hector and roughly put his hand on his shoulder in what Fred thought was a chummy gesture to make Hector feel at ease. It startled Hector and only interrupted the vent Hector was attempting to facilitate instinctively by his rhythmic rocking from front to back. He felt Fred's hand as it rubbed the soft cotton shirt, which Hector suffered as though it were an abrasive burlap/sandpaper sensation.

"Errrrrhaaa," Hector moaned.

Fred left his hand on Hector's shoulder and tightened his grip slightly, now trying to act like his macho pal, although Fred had no idea what Hector's concept of a friend could be.

"Hector, we have to get combs in the envelopes today, you only did one bin yesterday, the rest of the day all you did was rock, and how are you going to make any money?"

Hector's tortured shoulder began to burn like fire. "EEERRRRAAA," Hector moaned as he gritted his teeth and tried to endure the pain, hoping that Fred would soon let go.

"The boss said your work plan is three bins a morning," Fred droned.

RRRRRRRRRRRR ... MUMBLE ... MUMBLE … MUMBLE … FLICKER ... FLICKER ... MUMBLE ... FLICKER ... RRRRRRR ... RUB ... RUB …

"SAND PAPER ON MY SHOULDERS," Hector thought franticly to himself.

On some level, Hector thought Fred meant well, but he couldn't stand the auditory distress. Fred's voice seemed to modulate through Hector like a sonic weapon compounding his torment. Hector wanted his pain, and mounting trauma, to explode into little confetti bits, to dissipate onto infinitesimal tiny fragments and disappear onto a nonexistent wind. But Fred continued to drone on like a migraine headache. Fred gave Hector's shoulder a little shake as though they were close buddies.

"Come on Hector, let's get back to work, you'll make me look bad,"Fred said as kindly as he could.

RRR, MUMBLE ... FLICKER ... RUB … RUB ... GRIND, GRIND, GRIND…

"INTO MY SHOULDER—SCRAPE THE SKIN OFF MY SHOULDER LIKE A WIRE BRUSH DOWN TO THE BONE IN AN OPEN BLOODY WOUND!!!" Hector desperately thought as he tried to break through the wall of pain and frustration, but all to no avail.

All of a sudden an ungovernable explosion of emotion which manifested itself in a physical reaction crested and surged over the banks of his restraint. Hector sprung out of his chair, easily shrugging off Fred's hand as though it were a child's. The chair crashed to the floor and Hector began to jump up and down. He slapped himself violently in the head with both hands.

"EEEEEEEE—EEEEEEEE—EEEEEEE," he screamed.

Fred forgot all his SCIP (Strategies for Crisis Intervention and Prevention) training and tried to grab Hector's wrists to stop him. Down came Hector's elbow and accidentally struck Fred's upper arm with a vicious blow. Fred backed off, angrily holding the offended appendage while it throbbed with hot agony as though someone had hit him with a ball peen hammer.

As Hector's behavior frantically increased, some of his fellow indentured servants were beginning to react to Hector's episode. This escalated the noise level in the room, agitating others. And they in turn began to join in and act out more or less in sympathy.

"AAAAAAAAAAAAA," screamed one skinny brown haired 20-something woman who was also autistic.

"SHUT UP—SHUT UP—SHUT UP," another individual started to tell the browned haired young lady.

Things were starting to look like a proverbial insurrection-rebellion. The fridge across the room kicked on again. RRRRRR-RRRRRRRRRR—and the lights continued their— FLICKER—FLICKER—FLICKER …

"AAAAAAAAAAAAA," went the brown haired autistic woman again,

"HA HA HA HA HA," laughed an individual that seemed to find great humor in the situation.

All this induced further agony to Hector's already over-loaded senses. His actions became more frantic, more violent.

"**Connie,** come in here, **Hector's** losing it again," Fred shouted impatiently, almost in a frenzy himself.

Connie, the supervisor, poked her head and shoulders into the room. Shaking her head at the mounting pandemonium she mumbled to herself. She proceeded over to the obvious source of the disturbance. She almost casually initiated a two-person escort which then helped Fred regain his own composure somewhat, and he then was able to complete the SCIP move properly.

They guided Hector as he aggressively struggled, and with great difficulty, out of the workroom toward a 'time-out' room. On the way, Connie looked at Fred with worry.

"What happened?" Connie asked in her heavy Jamaican accent. "Hector was in a good mood this morning, he was even happy when I saw him." Pointedly she looked at Fred, waiting.

"I don't know," Fred grunted out as he struggled with Hector, "he just went off when I asked him to put his combs into the packaging."

Fred was trying to regain his macho composure; his ego was wounded in that he could not handle one '*window licker*' was what he thought to himself concerning Hector while he and Connie moved Hector down the hallway toward the cubicle.

All of a sudden, as if Hector heard the unspoken insult by Fred, he planted his feet and surged to one side shoving Fred into the sharp corner of a wall.

"Ouch, you fuckin' retard," Fred bellowed.

"Watch it, that's enough of that," Connie warned.

"He hurt my shoulder. I should go for workman's comp," Fred complained.

Connie looked at Fred and rolled her eyes, her accent became more defined. "Oh you poor baby mahn—going ta' try to get another three weeks off, why don't you just go on welfare then they can just mail you your paychecks."

"That's not a bad idea," Fred shot back sarcastically.

They had this discussion over Hector's verbalization of 'EEEEEEEEEEEE' and momentarily arrived at the cubicle and put Hector still tense, and struggling to slap his head, inside-alone.

"If he calms down in 15, there's only an hour left in the morning anyway, maybe he'll be better after lunch," Connie breathed almost to herself.

Fred just looked at Connie and gave his best plastic smile.

"Yeah, whatever you say, you're the boss."

Connie gave him a steely warning glare and went the opposite way down the hallway.

"That's it," ... she thought to herself, *"this one is gone ... all I need is a paper trail and he's gone."*

Fred turned to go back to the workroom.

"Fuckin' retard," Fred muttered under his breath as he rubbed his arm, "Screw them I'm going to the nurse to fill out an injury report, let them work short staffed with those stamp-lickers." Fred continued on past the workroom and proceeded on to the nurse and happily took an unscheduled 30 minute break.

Hector was sitting in the cubicle with four walls, no windows and a door with a little wire-impregnated peek-a-boo glass set at eye level.

"EEEEEEEE," Hector screamed.

He was trying to regain his composure. The many, horrible sensations that had assaulted him were beginning to subside. The room was less intrusive, physically and emotionally, than where he had been. At least the physical pain and emotional torment from the previous events were beginning to decrease.

Hector stood alone in the room smack, smack, smack, slapping himself in the head as he contemplated what happened. Trying with this violent act against his person, to focus his command, his self control; to regain any mastery over himself that he could manage. The fury of his outburst was subsiding. The self-abuse of striking himself had helped him focus. He stopped slapping himself and began to rock—violently at first. Soon the fervor of the rocking combined with the additional self taught coping skill of tapping his chest rhythmically with his right hand began its work, its magic, much as meditation was for some, prayer for others, or tapping fingers on a desk for yet others. Instinctual or learned, the source of these forms of diversion didn't matter. The effect was similar. The room was much quieter than the workroom. Not perfect, but better. Hector could still hear things in the room next to him.

People talking in low voices...

"He's over there again, huh?" they said about him.

But the sounds were muffled, and thankfully the light was was smaller and not as intense as the 50-plus fluorescent lights, each with their individual dual set of bulbs flickering simultaneously. He could no longer hear the rrrrrrrrrrrrrrr of the refrigerator or the screams and mumble … mumble … scream of those around him. The violent rocking he was performing began to abate as his commitment to the coping skill began to yield fruit.

A decrease of the fervor of his episode became apparent. Within several minutes Hector's actions had slowed to a soothing rhythm. Hector began to think as rationally as he could. He felt mortified for the umpteenth time in his life. Mortified that he could not get through the anguish of a confrontational situation, as he had been able to do on better days. This humiliated him. Another personal tempest, one of thousands through the many years, had occurred and passed. Leaving Hector drained physically and emotionally. And this time, as with many others, Hector had failed—again—and he was ashamed. Wondering why he could not be as those around him, Hector felt very alone in the universe. Hector rocked back and forth, staring beyond the four walls for a consolation he could not find in his transient cell.

It was lunchtime at Hector's facility. The attendants scurried about assisting the disabled adults in finding their lunches and getting them settled in to eat.

Ike opened his lunch box and took out his sandwich. For long moments he just stared, then with his slow customary speech pattern.

"Godd daaamn iiitt, I hate mayonnaise," Ike murmured.

This type of blue language gave Ike great pleasure, as his mother always reacted with a very satisfying grimace on her face and would tell him that he was being vulgar. Ike liked the sound of that word. 'Vulgar'. It meant he had power over his mother that she never realized she had given him, and due to her own neurosis, she was never able to take away. Also, Ike had had mayonnaise every day for the last week, and Samantha (at the house), told him if he didn't like it he didn't have to eat his lunch. Ike got angry when he thought of Samantha.

"If you don't like it —don't eat it," she would tell him when he would ask her if he could have yellow mustard.

It's not so much that he didn't like mayonnaise; it's just that he didn't like Samantha treating him like his mother used to when he lived at home.

Ike pondered this for a few crucial moments. Suddenly he threw his sandwich back over his head. Fred happened to be strolling past as Ike's sandwich flew past his nose only centimeters away. It startled him just as he was finally beginning to get his equilibrium back from this morning's episode with Hector. Fred looked over and saw Ike's defiant expression.

"That's it, Ike!" Fred spat. "Every day this week you have thrown your sandwich. You don't want to eat, fine!"

"I hate mayonnaise," Ike said under his breath. All he heard in his head was Samantha,

"Don't like it, don't eat it—don't like it, don't eat it—don't like it, don't eat it..."

"**Pick up** that sandwich Ike," Fred sputtered. "I'm not cleaning up after you again."

Ike automatically began to struggle out of his chair; his coordination certainly was not that of an athlete, to say the very least. He was finally on his feet as Fred glared at him. At first all Ike saw were Fred's ears turning red. He began to turn to go get the sandwich, as he'd always done in the past when given an order from the Freds, or Samanthas, or the many others like them, wherever he's lived or worked over the years. Then all of a sudden he stopped. Ike looked down at his feet—his slow cognitive process ticked off the seconds—then something in his psyche clicked in, and quietly but defiantly, Ike voiced one word...

"No!!!"

Fred couldn't believe his ears, which by the way began to turn even redder, if that was possible.

"W-W-What, did you say?" Fred stuttered incredulously, as though his tongue wouldn't work properly.

Ike looked Fred in the eye.

"Nooo Fred, nooo God Daaamn it," Ike drawled out in his characteristically slow speech.

Ike smiled to himself at being vulgar and this apparent small victory over 'the man'. (Something he had seen in a movie recently. *'Don't let the man keep you down'* the actor in the movie said.)

Fred almost went cross-eyed and his ears looked as though they would explode.

"That's it, Ike. I've had enough of your guys' shit today, I'm calling the house, and you can go home now, see how much your paycheck will be this week. But first pick up that fuckin' sandwich."

Other people look over at the disturbance. No regular was close enough to hear what Fred said to Ike.

Ike raised his fist up to his jaw, pointed his index finger at Fred, squinted his eyes, and said the first thing he could think of to threaten Fred.

"Yoooouuu—youuu'rre **fired!**"

Connie came up behind Ike as he continued his open confrontation with Fred, touched him on the shoulder. "Come on Ike, that's enough," she spoke in a firm but low-key voice.

Ike tried to spin around to give Connie some of his new found bluster, since he was on a roll. But he caught his feet in the chair legs, tripped and accidentally lunged toward Connie. She screamed in surprise and retreated backward as Ike stumbled after her seemingly on the attack. Fred grabbed Ike in a half nelson, and using Ike's already considerable downward momentum put him to the floor none too gently.

"AAAAAA," moaned Ike loudly in pain and disgrace. "I don't like mayonnaise," he muttered as his face was pushed onto the floor.

"Easy on him," Connie warned Fred.

"You saw him try to attack you," Fred retorted as he was holding down a defenseless moaning Ike. Do you want to end up with an injury?"

"He surprised me, but he's no Bruce Lee you know," Connie shot back . "Now let him up!!!" she ordered, pinning Fred with the 'Hairy Eye Ball'.

Fred looked up at her for an instant; then got off of Ike.

Connie helped Ike up from the floor so that he could catch his breath.

"I'll tell Elmer on you Fred. I hate mayonnaise!!" Ike screamed out of fear and anger.

He tried to strike Fred with a spastic overhand slap. Fred blocked the assault easily. Just then Connie stepped in and applied the appropriate SCIP methods to Ike, getting him in a single-person escort.

"**Connieee,**" Ike bellowed in humiliation.

She almost nonchalantly took a complaining Ike out of the program room and down the hall out of sight before others in the room began another insurgency.

Fred and the other staff were left to restore peace to the room, which began to calm down with the major stimulus gone from the area. Ike would be safely confined where he could no longer instigate the others into another riotous episode.

Minutes later, Ike was in the very same time-out room which had previously housed Hector, and Fred was in the workshop office on the phone calling Elmer at Ferris House.

Elmer, who had made the mistake of thinking he would get a lot of paperwork done today, answered the office phone to Fred's mocking tone.

"What's with your people today?" Fred queried, happy to have someone to take his frustration out on … someone that he could feel superior to today besides '*these tar tar's that I work with'*...was one of the thoughts flowing through his brain at that instant. "Two out of three of your people were or are in my time-out room so far this morning," he boldly finished.

Elmer was silent on the other end of the phone, still trying to place the voice.

Fred started to get braver. "What the hell is going on at that house of yours that these guys are bringing such hostility to work with them? Ike actually attacked Connie." Fred paused, feeling happy with his effort that effectively shifted any guilt that may have been lurking in the back of his mind to Disabled People of America, Inc. and one of their representatives. Also, he enjoyed putting someone else on the spot. Fred left a pregnant silence thinking to intimidate Elmer.

Elmer began to realize that it was Fred, that schmuck from program who should be working in a factory and not with the disabled. Also Elmer was dubious, to say the least, and not easily intimidated.

"Ike attacked Connie? What happened? I can't possibly imagine Ike getting physical with anyone. Maybe verbal... But never physical; and I've known him for four years, even before he moved to this house from our campus, Fred, and that kind of behavior is as out of character for him as it is for you."

Elmer couldn't see but Fred's ears were beginning to turn red on the other side of the phone. This was not going the way he had anticipated. Elmer's voice broke in on his concentration.

"Did anything else happen that you know of, Fred … something that could have preceded this brutal, violent, outburst of Ike's?" Elmer queried with mock incredulity.

There was a momentary silence from the other side of the phone.

"I-I-I don't know," Fred stammered…

Fred was losing ground fast—his ears were now glowing like red Christmas lights. He was relieved no one else had come into the room to see his embarrassment. He was angry at being put on the defensive so easily.

"He just threw his lunch and went off," Fred lamented.

"Did he come back on?" Elmer asked.

Elmer was getting tired of Fred, whom he had seen at program before, on previous midday stops for I.S.P. (Individual Service Plan) meetings with Connie. And Elmer had not been impressed with his demeanor. Another silence ensued from the other end of the phone. Elmer wondered if Fred even understood his attempt at sarcasm.

"I'm leaving now," Elmer finally muttered in a resigned voice. "I'll be there in about," Elmer looked at his watch, "twenty minutes, to pick them up. Oh yeah I'll need a complete incident report on both of these episodes along with any injury reports from your R.N. on duty today, and thanks in advance."

Elmer hung up the phone without saying goodbye. Fred said goodbye to a dead line so that anyone within earshot didn't know that he had been hung up on, and that he had also lost the battle of wits with Elmer. Of course Fred never realized that he had gone into battle unarmed.

This was the same reason some thought he was not good for this type of work and should probably seek employment in a factory. But this was not what Fred was thinking as he went back to work. He was thinking more along the lines of someone that blamed disabled people for being the way they are, while not realizing that he likely had the more profound disability.

A half an hour later, Elmer was sitting in an office talking to Fred. Elmer looked directly into Fred's watery brown eyes. All Elmer saw was an individual who had very little insight and less compassion, and should be pumping gas somewhere, but certainly not working with people less able. He saw the look of a person that was bored with what they did at their job, and was truly only there for a paycheck.

"What set him off, Fred?" Elmer inquired.

"I don't know, he just threw his sandwich and started acting like an asshole," Fred said a little too quickly.

Elmer did not address this statement but made a mental note to speak to Connie, who he knew was good at what she did, and moved on.

"You didn't notice anything with his behavior? He didn't say anything? No one was antagonizing him? You didn't notice any of the usual triggers?"

"Nothing that I noticed," Fred stated innocently. "What do you think I am? I would never let something upsetting happen to my people and not address it—that would be neglect," he said smugly. "Look lunch is over and I have to get back into the work area. I have a lot of workers to supervise. You know where to pick up your people." Fred left the office thinking he had done an exemplary job once again.

Elmer briefly contemplated what just occurred. He knew from experience that this potential abuse was not over and that he had to pursue the occurrences over a period of time to conclude the events of today. He reflected to himself, '*paper trail*'. He knew he owed this to Hector and Ike.

Elmer proceeded down the hall to a sitting room where Hector and Ike were waiting. Hector was gently rocking back and forth; Ike was sitting mumbling something about damned mayonnaise, along with some other more creative expletives, and smiling, very pleased with something.

Elmer walked in the room. "How's it going guys? Guess we had a bad morning."

Hector ran over to Elmer, grabbed his hand and started pulling him toward the door. Ike got up and walked over towards the door.

"Hi Elmer," Ike drawled out sluggishly, relief apparent in his voice. "I want to go home, I'm hungry."

Ike knew he was safe with Elmer. He had never been treated badly by Elmer since he had known him. He considered Elmer a friend.

As they left the building Elmer looked at the both of them

"It must be getting near a full moon or something," he thought to himself.

In the car on the way home, Ike kept thinking to himself. *"I hate mayonnaise, tastes like shit. They always give me mayonnaise. Why can't they give me bologna and cheese? I like bologna & cheese."*

The car hummed along.

"Elmer, can I have some bologna and cheese when we get home?" Ike questioned almost lethargically.

Hector gently rocked back and forth in the back seat with a little smile on his face and tapped his chest with his right hand, seemingly very relaxed.

"Sure Ike we'll stop at Tony's store on the way home."

Shortly the car pulled into the parking lot at Tony's convenience store.

"So Ike, why did you throw your lunch?" Elmer broke into Ike's thoughts.

"I-I-I don't knooow," Ike said, slowly modulating his words up, and then back down the scale.

"You must have some idea, Ike. That's the third time in less than two weeks. You're not going to make any money for your vacation at this rate."

"I know, Elmer, I'm sorry," Ike stated remorsefully.

Hector was continually rocking back and forth, casually, seemingly happy just to be in the car.

Elmer continued the conversation.

"There must be some reason, Ike. You can tell me; I'm your buddy, right?" Elmer asked conspiratorially.

"Yes, Elmer you're my buddy."

"Well, spill it pal, what's the word?"

Ike considered for several long moments, then he finally relented. “I had mayonnaise in my lunch and I don’t like mayonnaise.”

“You weren’t supposed to have mayonnaise, Ike. I’ll speak to Samantha again.” Elmer didn’t notice the look on Ike’s face at the mention of Samantha’s name.

“This time we’ll make sure you get bologna and cheese. We’re at the store right now. Let’s go pick some up,” Elmer trailed off as he parked the car. Elmer turned off the engine and all three men went into the store. Hector automatically grabbed a soda from the cooler. A young woman in her twenties, with a little boy approximately four years old, desperately pulled the child away from the aisle where the soda coolers were, firing an apprehensive glance at Hector.

“Hector, the sodas are colder in the other cooler, I just stocked those.

The elderly balding man behind the counter spoke up. Hector put the soda back, wandered over to the other cooler and grabbed a new soda.

Ike waved to the man behind the counter in his usual Ike-slow-motion manner, “Hi, Tony!”

Tony gave Ike the thumbs up. “You guys are a little early today.”

“Yeah,” Ike spoke sheepishly.

Tony looked at Ike thoughtfully, with a little smile on his face. “Half a pound of bologna, half a pound of cheese, Ike?”

“Yeah Tony, American cheese,” Ike’s face brightened.

“Make it a pound of both,” Elmer put in.

“Comin’ right up,” Tony said, as he got to work behind the counter.

Tony struck up a conversation with Elmer as he sliced the cold cuts.

“So Elmer, where’s the rest of the house?”

“Still at work Tony, what do I owe you for this stuff?”

“$12.37,” Tony answered.

Elmer took out the money and put it on the counter.

“Thanks Tony.”

“Thaaanks Tony,” Ike repeated.

Hector was opening his soda and crooning with pleasure. As they proceed towards the exit, the woman and her child came up to the check-out. She glared at Tony behind the counter.

"I don't feel safe with him in here with my son."

She nodded her head toward Hector's back as he departed.

"You shouldn't allow them in here."

As Tony rung her up, he patiently took a breath.

"They're not so bad lady, give 'em a chance."

"I can shop down the street," she snapped vehemently.

She harrumphed as she took her bag and headed toward the door.

Tony gazed up to heaven as she exited. "Thank God for small favors," he mumbled under his breath.

Later, back at the house, the evening crew started coming in shortly before Sally and Abigail arrived home from program. Nancy had already left for the day.

Elmer sat in the office and spoke to Jenn. "Do me a favor, Jenn," he asked. "Tell Samantha to make Ike's sandwich with bologna and cheese for Monday with NO mayonnaise, or I'll call her at home the next time he creates a disturbance and she can go pick him up."

"Fat chance," Jenn laughed. "You'll never get her back out of her bed once she's home. How's everyone else doing?"

"Hector was upset, too. I had to pick them both up by Lunch time, and God only knows what set off Hector," Elmer had a troubled look as he though of Fred.

"I wonder why? He's been in a good mood lately," Jenn looked thoughtful.

"With some of the people at the workshop and their fascist attitude, I'm sure I'd go off too," Elmer said tiredly.

Jenn looked closely at Elmer. "You look like you had a long day, boss. Why don't you go home?"

As Elmer headed for the door, he presented a tired smile.

"I'd like to," he said. "But I have to run to campus and do a late day class for the new trainees. Say, come to think of it, Chico wanted to email his friend in the Shawnee House. Why don't you or David get him started after dinner while the others are watching TV, or relaxing, or otherwise occupied?"

"OK boss," she said cheerfully. "That sounds like it will be fun. Have a good class."

"Why not," Elmer declared tiredly as he walked out the door.

Jenn, Abigail and Sally were taking the dishes and cheap silverware from the cabinets in the kitchen and were in the process of setting the table for supper. David, another swing shift employee at Ferris House, was busy assisting Chico in removing the tuna casserole from the oven.

They heard Ike in the background talking to Hector.

"Nooo Hector, Dave said we have to use soap when we wash our hands."

Absentmindedly, David spoke over his shoulder into the other room,

"Come on Hector, and use soap."

"Heee is Dave," Ike defended Hector from the bathroom.

"Soups on," Chico piped up to anyone within earshot, as he and David carried the food to the table.

Hector shot out of the downstairs bathroom and into the dining room as Ike lumbered casually after him. Everyone sat themselves in the same chairs they were at for breakfast. David and Jenn assisted them in making their plates. As soon as they got their food, they started shoveling it in.

"Don't you guys want any juice with your dinner?" Jenn asked.

She moved the pitchers of juice in front of them and they haphazardly poured their own juice. David and Jenn then began to serve themselves plates of food and sat at the table to eat with the rest.

As the meal progressed, typical dinner-time conversation ensued.

"Dave," Chico piped up, "Hector and Ike got in trouble at work today. B-b-both of them got in trouble Dave."

"Shut up Chico," Ike mumbled ominously around a mouthful of food as he attempted to devour his share.

Hector and the others concentrated on their food as though they were stone deaf.

"You should stick to your own concerns," David informed gently, trying to avoid a situation.

"I know Dave," Chico answered slowly.

For some unknowable reason Clark chimed in adding salt to the wound. "He threw his lunch and he told Fred, 'Fuck you'."

"Now, we don't use such language at the dinner table," Jenn interjected.

All of a sudden Ike hollered out.

"I-I-I-I don't like mayonnaise, **I-I-I-I don't like mayonnaise**," Ike started to get excited, spraying food from his mouth. "I always get mayonnaise."

Everyone else continued to eat as though nothing was happening, not out of embarrassment, which would be a normal reaction for regulars. This type of reaction was a coping skill, meant to protect their respective plates of food. Ingrained into them from institutional life, it would take a bomb to distract the others.

Dave tried to distract him before he escalated further, beyond the point of no return.

"So you guys went to the store, huh?" David continued. "Did you see Tony?"

Ike was still agitated but began to focus on David.

"Yeah, Tony," Ike declared, with a strange mixture of anger and enthusiasm.

"What did you buy at the store, Ike?" David asked evenly, as he took another fork of tuna casserole and calmly put it in his mouth.

"We bought bologna and cheese," Ike moaned out.

Ike was getting more into the present moment and began to get past his irritation —his somewhat delayed stress from lunch time.

"Oh good," Jenn said. "That's what we can make your lunch with."

"And Nooo mayonnaise," Ike shouted, starting to remember why he was pissed-off.

Chico started snickering.

Sally smiled and innocently asked. "Can I have bologna and cheese too?"

"No, that's what I'm having." Ike interjected as if no one else could have what he was going to have for lunch.

"I'm sure there will be plenty," David remarked.

Sally smiled to herself contentedly and continued to eat.

"Now, let's finish eating so we can have some dessert. And yes, Ike no mayonnaise," David finished before Ike refocused on the hot button issue of the moment.

At length the 'D' word refocused everyone's attention and they finished out the meal peacefully, if not neatly.

After dinner, after all were finished with their evening chores … while the other residents of the house were busy either watching TV or … in Hector's case lurking around the backyard, Chico hesitantly approached Jennifer.

"Jenn?" Chico timidity inquired.

"Yes Chico," Jenn answered only half listening as she was distracted somewhere else, in this case a goals chart.

"Can I e-mail Chucky?"

"It's not e-mail, Chico, it's Instant Messenger, and David will get you going with it after everyone cleans up," she said absentmindedly.

David was at the other desk in the office and without looking up from his paperwork overheard, and expanded on the conservation.

"Only if you have done everything you are listed to do as chores tonight, could you check on the rest?" David asked Jenn.

"No problem," she looked up from the goal chart she was working on. "It's easier than teaching Chico to type."

David smiled at Chico, and noticed he had an abject look on his face from the unintended hurt of Jenn's comment. "We're doing good typing, right Chico?"

Chico looked at Dave happily. "Yeah Dave, good typing huh? Better than Jenn," Chico taunted Jenn in a friendly fashion.

Jenn smiled and, shook her head as she went into the living room to check on Sally and Abigail.

"So, how was your day ladies?" she inquired.

Abigail ignored her and continued to watch TV.

"My day was good," Sally said as she smiled and looked up from a book on dogs she was enjoying. "They always rush me though," she slowly spilled out her unease. "They say ***come on, come on, let's go*** you're going too slow." As she imitated 'them' she waived her hands in an almost comical manner. "I like working but sometimes I think they're mad at me."

"Well, did you do something to get them mad at you?" Jenn looked at her with a mommy-dearest-you-should-feel-guilty look.

Sally looked down at her book ashamedly. She was obviously embarrassed although she didn't know why.

Jenn got a reproachful tone in her voice, "What did you do?"

David entered the room, catching enough of the conservation, and cut in,

"Lay off her, Jenn," David's voice was almost too quiet.

Jenn didn't see David come into the room.

"She probably didn't do anything more than ask to go to the bathroom."

Sally looked up from her book almost defiantly. "I think they get mad with me. I don't want to get them mad at me." Sally began to well up with tears. "I don't want them to not like me."

"Oh I don't think they're upset, dear," David put in. "Maybe they're just preoccupied. I'm sure you do just fine. You're too nice to upset anyone," He continued in a consoling voice.

Ike, who was all cleaned up from dinner, was now sitting in another easy chair across the living room. He began to chuckle.

David told Ike in the same calm low-tone voice but not with as much edge as with Jenn, "It's not funny Ike, we didn't laugh at you with what happened to you today, now did we?"

"Nooo Daave," Ike drawled out his speech again ending almost a half an octave lower at the end of David's name than at the beginning of the word no. "I'm sorrryy, Saallly," Ike declared.

"That's good," Sally returned happily, as she began to brighten up. "You're still my friend, Ike. I have fun at work … I like going there ... my team leader … says if I do real good ... I can move on to the next part and move to the workshop... I can make money there."

All these proclamations came out in the slow halting speech of a person struggling under the yoke of having a functional I.Q. of maybe 79.

"That's right sweetheart," Jenn said, changing her tone as well as her demeanor while she remembered how she should be dealing with the situation.

Sometimes she had to remind herself that she was working with adults who deserve the same respect she did. Not with her children at home where she can treat them with a different tack. Not that Jenn was a bad person; sometimes people just don't think.

"You should be able to handle that fine," Jenn continued. "You've learned a lot in the time you've worked there. Come on, lets watch some TV with Abigail." Jenn coaxed Sally in an appeasing fashion.

Abigail hummed to herself, showing no reaction, apparently mesmerized by the television.

"Or you can show me your dog book," Jenn encouraged.

"Look at the … dog ... I … want," Sally happily got out.

David went into the office, leaving the four in the living room. Chico was at the computer desk waiting eagerly for him.

"Hi Dave, lets g-g-go," Chico stuttered in his excitement.

"All right keep your shirt on," David smiled with a trace of humor in his voice.

David and Chico booted up the computer. As David brought up the instant messenger, Ike's friend's nickname, Chucky, came up as being online. "Chico and the Man, ar you home?" Chucky's message asked.

David handed the keyboard over to Chico and helped Chico place his fingers on the keyboard.

"Just like we practiced Chico," David said, "take your time, there's no rush."

"Hi chucky, how was waz yer day?" Chico very slowly typed back. *Enter.*

After long moments a message came back.

"Hi Chico I had a good day I went too the docktor today for blud wrok I got ice kreme after that," Chucky's message read.

Chico took time to try to read the message. David helped him patiently.

"What do you say to that Chico?" Dave inquired.

"That's pretty good. You should get me ice cream when I go for blood work, huh Dave?" Chico plied.

"You always want ice cream, Chico. I should call you the ice cream man."

Chico smiled at David and went back to the computer.

Hector came into the room, all cleaned up for bed and began to rock slowly back and forth in his pajamas.

"Hi Hector," David said absentmindedly.

He helped Chico correct some things on the next message. Chico tapped the enter key and sent the message. With great satisfaction he rubbed his hands together like a happy miser.

"Ok then, do you need me any more, or do you think you have the hang of it?" David asked.

"I can do it, Dave," Chico beamed , "I know how."

"Good, I have some paper work to do. Don't forget to turn off the computer if you get tired before I get back." David left the office.

For the next hour Chico and Chucky from Shawnee House slowly communicated back and forth about how their day went.

"Its payday today Chucky I made 87$s an 58 sents," typed Chico. *Enter*.

It took a while, and then Chucky's message came back.

"I didn't make tat much. I had to Docktors apponts this weak. Shau Shing took me i like him he's my friend." The message read.

Chico took a good five minutes to compose and send his message.

"I lik Dave to hes my friend," *Enter,* Chico tapped the key.

Chico waited patiently for the next message. Hector watched from the corner of the room, still rocking gently. Chico looked over to Hector for a moment.

"Hi buddy?" Chico smiled .

Hector looked at Chico and tapped his chest twice as though in acknowledgement as he continued to rock. Although Hector was nonverbal he and Chico had built a firm bond over the months since they had been thrust together.

The next message came in from Chucky.

"I like Shau-Shing to he does not yell at me like Fernando does Hes my friend to. Iwish they could leave me alone I am never alone always staf are here."

Chico read the message slowly and started to tap his chin with his index finger like he had seen his father do on their recent visit. The gesture on him looked comical to those that have known him for any length of time, almost as though they thought he should not be capable of seemingly normal behavior or mannerisms.

Chico was starting to get tired, but pushed on to compose one more message before signing off.

"The only leave me alone when I visit my father Or else they are always around. I am getting tired Chucky and no wok tomorrow. Good night Chucky we are going bowlin tomorrow." *Enter.*

Chucky sent his good-byes a few minutes later.

Chico got up from the computer and looked over to Hector.

"Come on, its time to go to bed, Hector."

Hector ignored him and continued to rock.

"Come on, let's go!" Chico tried to grab Hector's hand but Hector pulled away and started to slap his head.

"S-S-Suit yourself. Stay here all night if you want, I'm going to bed."

Chico gave a lion's yawn and walked out, leaving the computer on, but he turned off the light.

Hector just stared at the computer screen as it was the only light in the room. Mesmerized he went over and stood in front of it rocking back and forth staring for some time, crooning with apparent pleasure...

4
The Weekend Visitor (Another Mouth to Feed)

All of Ferris House breathed a sigh of relief; the next day was Saturday. Children who were torn away from their TV sets or their video games and kicked out of doors were riding their bicycles up and down the roads. Or to the downtown area not too distant for their youthful energies. Nearby, others were playing ball in a ball field with an old half-rusted beat up back stop.

Adults were out cutting their lawns or washing their vehicles. Mr. Edmondson, who was an alcoholic used-car salesman at an auto mall in the next town, was painting his house. He was not happy doing this but his wife had been harping about this project all spring. So he painted. They had all but forgotten about the town hall incident and the retards that lived at Ferris House.

"It's getting hot already, I could use a beer," Mr. Edmondson was thinking to himself.

He slipped into the kitchen, past the room where his wife was shopping online and grabbed a couple of beers.

"She's always on that damn computer," he thought as he stealthily crept back past her. *"Still got it,"* he congratulated himself as he tiptoed back to his chore outside, not disturbing her. *"Quiet as a burglar,"* he mused with glee. He popped his beer and resumed his chore; he would be plastered by mid- afternoon, long before his wife got off the computer for a snack.

Marc Ferris, brother to the famous John Ferris, the double-crosser that sold 350 Ferris Road to those chin- slobberers, was out preparing his field for summer cabbage. He had a small produce stand on the road, more to keep busy than to make money. He and his wife Joan had worked in the state mental health system locally in one of the counties' state hospitals until they were 55 and able to take their tier one retirement.

Joan was 59 with dark auburn hair beginning to streak with gray, and light blue eyes. Her husband, Marc, always told her she was too beautiful to marry a farmer.

Although she agreed with him, she fell in love with him anyway. Her family, who were big money people in the area, would have preferred Joan marry at least into her peer group, but that did not happen as love goes where it's sent, even in a dung heap. Her family eventually accepted Marc, especially when he inherited a good portion of land from his father and became a land millionaire.

Marc and Joan tried to have children right away, as was the dictate of society in those days. At first they had little success, but eventually they did have a son. One of life's cruel dealings left their son, Marc Jr. a sickly child. At the age of five years old, Marc Jr. was diagnosed with leukemia. The Ferris' experienced all the horrors of fighting childhood cancer that a young family could. Their beloved child passed on at the tender age of seven. But they were strong people that were deeply in love, and their marriage survived the tragedy.

Many of these experiences from so long ago would occasionally surface to haunt Joan. To keep these specters at bay, she performed one of her favorite pastimes. She was in her main flower garden working with her prize roses. This was always a great joy to her and over the years had brought her much serenity. It had helped to ease her sorrowful state of mind, creating her own private respite.

As she worked pulling weeds and mulching where needed, a sudden uneasiness intruded on her calm, that strange creepy feeling a person got when someone had crept up behind them and was standing too close. Invading their personal space, making the skin on the back of their neck crawl.

Joan suddenly stood up and turned around. Instinctively, following her intuition, she scanned the shrubs on the property line. Eventually she saw Hector, still as stone, behind the large forsythia. Being a friendly neighbor type, she started over to say hello, but by the second step in Hector's direction, Hector suddenly took off like a jackrabbit and, in less than a split second disappeared through the rear entrance of his house. Joan turned back to her roses …

"I guess he's just shy," she thought to herself. She soon forgot about Hector as she became re-immersed into her garden and thoughts of what might have been.

Meanwhile, inside Ferris House, Ike was hungry.

"Good morning Darla," he drawled out. Ike paused for more than a few beats while his soggy brain formulated the next appropriate question. "What's for breakfast?" he finally asked.

Darla went from the coffee pot over to the griddle, which was already hot; she checked the heat control again.

"What would you like, Ike?" she asked kindly.

Once again Ike kicked his thought process into high-gear trying to think through enough medication to put most people in a mild coma. This was like thinking through fuzzy molasses. But for Ike and most of the others living at Ferris House, who had been on these medication therapies for decades, it was a restraint to which they had become accustomed.

All of a sudden his face brightened up and he happily blurted out. "Eggs!" he exclaimed victoriously.

"Ok,"Darla sang as she prepped the griddle unnecessarily for the fourth time, causing one to wonder if she herself suffered from an obsessive compulsive personality. "Why don't you get some out of the fridge?"

Through all of this, Samantha performed her favorite pastime and shoveled enough food for three people from her plate into her mouth. She developed a slight scowl as she pretended to ignore the interchange, and continued to do the paperwork which sat on the table beside her plate of food. She was envious of the relationship that Darla so easily developed with the people who lived at Ferris House. This also made her callus.

"Well, if you have this under control I'll go into the office to finish up my paper work." Samantha displayed a petulant air as she gathered up her books and high-tailed it toward the office before Darla could ask for help.

In the office Samantha went to the computer, which was still on from last night. "Wait till I tell that David about this," she bitched to herself. "It's that damn tar tar Chico; he shouldn't be allowed on the computer anyway," she grumbled under her breath.

She sat down and started to play on the computer herself. She spent a lot of her time on her computer at home as well. At Ferris House some had nicknamed her the computer nerd, as she was very good with computers. She had learned by utter, constant use, always with the mouse at work or at home clicking away.

By now, back in the kitchen, Sally and some of the others were also awake and having breakfast.

"What are we … gonna to do … today Darla?" Sally inquired smiling happily at Darla. "Are we going … for a ride?"

Darla smiled back as she poured herself some coffee and sat at the table beside Sally. "Not until we clean up the yard and cut the lawn; we don't have to have our house looking like tobacco road, do we now?" Darla looked at them all with raised eyebrows.

Everyone around the breakfast table took a little time to take this in. Finally Ike, not really being one for physical labor, piped up.

"I don't want to work in the yard Darla."

Darla looked kindly at Ike. "Do you like this house Ike?" she gently inquired.

Ike thought this over for a full ten seconds. "Yeah Darla I like it here," and then lower he declared to himself, 'my house'.

"Well we want to keep on the neighbors' good side don't we?" Darla's tone was still caring and patient.

"Yeah Darla," Ike stated slowly after thinking about this for several long moments.

"Well, I think we should all help each other clean up breakfast, and ourselves, and try to get the yard done by lunch time. After all we have to keep up with the Jones' so to speak," she suggested.

"Keep up with the Jones," Abigail mumbled to herself in a sing-song voice as she ate her breakfast.

Darla studied everyone around the breakfast table in turn.

"After all we want our house to look as good as the next door neighbors, don't we? Then we can go for a ride after lunch, ok?"

"Ok Darla," Ike stated absentmindedly as he turned back to his breakfast, apparently satisfied.

The others simply continued to eat, not yet awake enough from their personal medication hangovers to react too vibrantly. Darla continued to aid any and all that needed assistance in making their breakfast until everyone was fed, and then with the process of completing other tasks known as A.D.L.'s., (Activities of Daily Living). This included brushing their teeth, shaving, where necessary, and combing or brushing their hair. Samantha was nowhere to be found until everything was complete.

She then materialized as though she were some plump magical fairy.

"You should have called me, Darla. I didn't know everything was done," she said.

Darla looked at her incredulously, and then called her bluff

"You can get out the lawn mower and start to cut the part of the lawn the work crew doesn't do while I help everyone rake and such."

Caught off guard, Samantha could only agree or expose her true slackard self, which Darla was already well aware of from general experience.

"Ok,"Samantha smarmily answered. "If my back can handle it."

"What can your back handle?" Darla retorted a little curt, "If it's too much you can go out on disability again you know."

Samantha simply harrumphed and retreated out the back door toward the tool shed. Darla took a breath and attempted to keep a positive attitude with what already looked like a semi-crappy day with Samantha.

A short while later out in the yard everyone had a specific job. Hector held a bag of red bark mulch while Chico took hands full and haphazardly spread it around the shrubbery in the gardens. Hector gently rocked back and forth as he absentmindedly held the bag open for Chico and followed him around the front of the house, cheerfully making keening sounds. They had learned to work well together as a team in a short period of time. This was the first time either had been in a home type setting in decades but they and everyone else adjusted quickly to having their own space. Over near the dumpster, Clark and Darla were busy struggling into rubber gloves so they could clean up the trash strewn around the dumpster from the neighborhood cats. It seemed no matter how well closed the lids were, animals still were able to access the tasty trash. Clark, a lanky fellow with a baldhead and a small pot belly, slowly picked up trash and put it into a small trash bag that Darla was holding open as Ike lazily swept the small back patio with a stiff bristled push broom.

Abigail and Sally were up at the edge of the driveway pulling dead underbrush from under and around the shrubbery bordering the road.

Suddenly Sally saw something cowering under the shrub she was working on. She stopped working and peered under the shrub into the low ground cover and heard a low ominous growl which raised the hair on the back of her neck as though she were walking through a graveyard and had just seen a ghost. She dropped her rake and ran frantically, screaming like the hounds of hell were chasing her.

She sprinted over to Samantha who was smoking a cigarette and leaning on the handle of a lawn mower pretending to supervise the girls down at the edge of driveway.

"Samantha, Samantha, there is something in the bushes," she cried hysterically.

Samantha agitatedly, impatiently, took a long bored drag off of her cigarette, and exhaled the smoke through her nose with a huge sigh. "Sally it's probably a squirrel, go back and get the hell to work, it's getting too hot and I have paperwork to do."

But Sally was frantic, apparently ready to jump out of her skin.

"What's wrong Sally?" Darla's voice came from a short distance behind Samantha.

Darla was walking down the driveway from where she and Clark had been struggling with the trash trying to get it back into the dumpster. Over by the shrubbery Abigail was jabbing her into the shrubs as she mumbled to herself incoherently. "Bark,

bark, bark, woof, woof," everyone suddenly heard from under the shrub.

Darla rushed over to the shrubbery near Abigail and gently took a hold of Abigail's rake with one hand and calmed her down. Sally was trailing hesitantly behind her.

The others in the yard had noticed the commotion and started working their way toward the bushes adjoining the road. By the time everyone was gathered around the distraction in the front yard, Darla was on her knees half way into the shrubbery cooing.

"It's ok, it's alright, come on baby no one will hurt you," she crooned.

At this point even Samantha had lumbered over to see what was going on.

Darla turned and shushed everyone back. "Spread out, move back, give me some room, you'll scare her," she warned in a low steady tone.

The residents obediently took a step back. Samantha harrumphed indignation and sucked another drag off her cigarette. Darla went back under the bush gently enticing whatever was there until a few moments later she came out with a frightened mixed breed young dog. “GGRRRRRRRRRRRR Woof, woof,” suggested the dog.

Clark involuntarily took a step back with a look of deep trepidation on his face. “That dog wants to bite me,” he voiced his dread.

Abigail stared, dismayed and somewhat slack-jawed and started one of her tunes.

Sally smiled brightly with delight and clapped her hands together. “Can we keep her?” she asked.

Chico smiled happily and looked up at Hector. Hector was rocking gently, he reached up with his right hand and gently tapped his chest three or four times.

Ike got a big smile on his square face, ha ha’d once or twice and slowly drawled out, “loook aa dawg.”

Darla held the dog’s filthy leash tenderly as she cooed to it. “It’s ok, it’s alright. Don’t worry Clark she doesn’t bite,” Darla assured.

Clark shifted his weight nervously from one foot to the other. Darla held her left hand out to the dog open palm, as the dog was cowering with her tail between her legs growling low in her chest.

Just then Samantha stomped over to Darla and the dog.

“Just what we need, another mouth to feed,” she said stridently.

Suddenly the dog turned toward Samantha barking ferociously. Thank God Darla had a hold of the leash and acted quickly enough to restrain the beast. Samantha took a step back, scared but not stupid enough to say anything more to antagonize the animal.

“Good dog!” Darla said smiling cheerfully.

“That’s not funny Darla, that’s a vicious animal and it should be put down,” Samantha intoned in a low ominous voice.

“No she’s not, she’s just scared,” Darla smiled. “And a good judge of character evidently. Aren’t you girl?”

The dog stopped barking and heeled to Darla’s left leg, leaning heavily on her, instinctively putting all her faith in Darla’s presence. Darla began to stroke the dog’s head and back.

Some of the residents hesitantly gathered around and the dog started to wag her tail.

Sally put her hand out, palm up like she saw Darla do.

"Can we keep her?" Sally asked again. "She looks like the one in my dog book."

"Yeah can we keep her?" Chico chimed in?

The dog was happily licking Sally's face at this point and the tail wagging increased.

"I think that dog wants to bite me," Clark, still nervous, suggested to no one in particular.

Darla tilted her head to one side as she studied the dog. Thinking out loud she put forth to the general ether. "She seems to be a very good natured dog, but someone must be looking for her, and no Clark, she doesn't want to bite you," she again assured. Darla seemed distracted as she watched the dog's behavior.

"We can't have a dog; besides, this one is dangerous." this came from Samantha who still had not moved from her spot. She was noticeably afraid of the animal, but more afraid of the contemplative look on Darla's face.

By now Chico, Sally, and Ike were gathered around. They petted the dog now that she had rolled onto her side and was letting Sally rub her stomach.

"Other houses have dogs, I have dogs, lots of people have dogs Samantha," Darla insisted.

"We'll see about this," Samantha turned and stalked off, with an air of resentment about her.

"We first have to see if she's hungry and thirsty, then we can check with the shelters and the neighbors to see who is missing her," Darla uttered more to herself than those nearby.

By now Darla had dropped the leash and Ike was trying to throw a stick he'd found for the dog, with half a degree of success. The dog chased the stick and brought it back to everyone's delight. Clark even moved tentatively closer, still anxious but not wanting to be left out.

Darla took her cell phone from her belt and called Elmer at home. It took eight rings but Elmer finally answered.

"Hello?" She heard Elmer's bleary voice on the other end of the phone.

"Hello boss," Darla sang with a smile on her face.

"What happened?" Elmer said guardedly, is everyone alright?"

"Yes all are well, but we have a visitor," Darla intoned into the receiver.

"Oh no," Elmer mumbled dejectedly. "Who—" he tried to gather his wits. "Not the clinical coordinator again?" he asked in a resigned fashion.

"No," Darla laughed really enjoying herself. "We have a stray dog."

She heard a low. "Oh shit," from Elmer's end of the phone, not quite under his breath. He was not prepared. He was trying to assess a situation that he really never dreamed of and desperately wished he didn't have to address; Darla heard a long sigh from the other end of the phone, then Elmer got down to business.

"Did it bite anyone?" he asked with a flat affect in his voice.

"No," Darla answered. "She's a big baby, she scared the hell out of Samantha but that's a good thing. Other than that she likes everyone else. They want to keep her." Darla chuckled again only half trying to contain her good hearted enjoyment of the circumstances.

"Just what we need," Elmer grumbled. "Look, Darla, do what you have to do to find out who owns the dog and to keep everyone and the house safe. I need these two days off or I'll go nuts."

"Don't worry boss I'll handle it," Darla laughed having too much fun, "and I'll see you on Monday."

Darla pushed the off button on the cell phone. She had been watching the dog play with some of the residents of Ferris House. The dog was about 60 pounds with half floppy short ears and all black with a spot of white on her chest.

"*Maybe a lab-shepherd mix,*" Darla thought to herself. "*Oh well, the yard looks pretty good, I might as well get some of them ready to go to the humane society to start the process,*" she reflected again to herself. "*This is the best thing that could have happened to this house even if we can't keep her.*" She watched how everyone was responding to the dog as if they already owned her. "*I hope no one claims her,*" was her last thought as she went to break up the fun.

After lunch, Shadoe, as the dog had been christened, as well as Darla, Abigail, Sally, Chico, and Clark loaded into the van to drive to 'the pound' as Clark called it. He had really responded since Shadoe snuck over and licked his hand when he wasn't being vigilant. At the time he almost pooped his pants until he realized that Shadoe was kissing his hand and not biting him. Sally was nervous; she didn't want anything to happen to Shadoe.

"What if the owners don't come back for her?" she asked Darla timidly.

Darla smiled knowingly at her. "I know you would like to keep her; so would I, but there is a lot to consider. First, we'll take her to be checked out at the shelter and see if we can find her owners. If we don't we will have to have a meeting to see what the house wants to do."

Clark and Chico were listening very closely, finally Chico spoke up.

"I want to keep her, she's a good dog," he said.

"Yeah me too," Clark put in almost assertively.

Clark never spoke up about anything before. This was out out of character for him as he was a natural coward. Darla good-naturedly looked at all in the group making eye contact with everyone in turn so she knew she had their attention. Then she spoke.

"As I've said, one step at a time, I don't want you guys to get your hopes up. She has a leash on and probably got away from some little girl," Darla stated pointedly. As she drove the van out of the driveway the conversation trailed away from the only other listener not in the van but briefly within earshot.

Hector was standing at the edge of the driveway. Once the van was out of sight he shot over to the border of the property and watched for Joan Ferris, his auburn haired neighbor who should be working in her rose garden soon. Rocking back and forth he patiently began his vigil, he would stand there for hours if no one interrupted him looking for Joan Ferris.

Back in the house, Samantha, relieved that *'those retards are finally out of my hair,'* proceeded to the refrigerator and started to rummage around inside like a hungry bear, her other favorite hobby. Ike came into the kitchen and tried to reach past her to grab a yogurt cup.

"Hey cut it out," Samantha drove her elbow into Ike's side and shoved him back out of the way.

Ike grunted from the blow but this was also his favorite hobby and he remained steadfast. "But I'm hungry," Ike sluggishly stated.

"**GO** and clean up the living room, you already had breakfast," Samantha spit viciously.

Ike, still stinging from the day before and what happened with Fred at work paused for an instant. He began to slowly process the humiliation as it filtered through his brain. As he considered this affront Ike's brain formulated a reaction— ***mutiny***.

"So did yoouuu," Ike asserted, his speech marked with rising emotion.

"Shut-up and go clean the living room or I'll write you up in the daily log," Samantha barked back over her shoulder. Assuming Ike's compliance and her supremacy, she continued her foraging.

Ike rubbed his hands together in an agitated fashion while he organized a response. He pointed a finger at Samantha.

"**Yooouur fired**," Ike hollered victoriously.

"**You wish**," Samantha shouted harshly. She rounded on Ike in an alarming fashion. Ike had no time to react before she grabbed his shoulder, turned him around and forcefully propelled him into the direction of the living room. **"NOW MOVE!"** she yelled.

Ike all of a sudden found himself in the living room. Feelings of anger and disparagement overtook his psyche. He began to mumble to himself.

"OOHHH," talking to himself as he often did. "They said this is my house—**my house**—he moved his arms in an almost uncontrollable spastic fashion out of growing frustration and anger. He heard Samantha go back to the refrigerator. Although he couldn't articulate these feelings swiftly, he considered this act of arrogance an affront by Samantha.

For a long moment he just thought about these events … and slowly came to the conclusion that too many times in his life a despicable deed like this had been perpetrated on him. He was told that this was his house to live in with the others. He was told he had rights in his own house.

Ike thought back to his years on ward one in Letchworth Village twenty years ago. He would get packages from his mother before she died. They would have chocolate chip cookies or stuffed animals in them. The attendants would sometimes tell him he could only have them if he was good and did what he was told to do. Sometimes he didn't even know the packages arrived. Many times the attendants simply stole the Contents.

Until Oscar, a kindly old night shift attendant who transferred to his ward entered into Ike's life. Oscar would give the packages to Ike whenever they arrived, much to the chagrin to some of his fellow employees. He would save some of the stuffed animals for Ike when he could not sleep at night. Ike had nightmares which came on him almost every night, so Oscar never had to save these for long. These terrible nightmares were of things that would slip into his subconscious about the abuses he endured by some of the people he lived with, the stronger ones—the scary ones. Ike was not good at fighting back; he had impeded motor function, and of course this caused him to react with clumsy and slow movements. Couple this with the sedative effects of his many psychotropic medication and this would make Ike a sitting duck for physical attack, and other abuses even more monstrous which would befall him after the lights went out. For years these events tortured him—until recently with Fred, and now with Samantha.

Ike had had enough. Who knew what finally did it for Ike; maybe he was just tired of other people being mean to him, maybe it was too much TV. As Ike simmered, his reminiscent processes continued on to the next place he lived before Ferris House.

After his mother died, with no one to advocate for him. No one came to visit him anymore, the state administrators transferred him to another place. It was more of a holding tank for institutionalized retarded and mentally ill people at another state-run institution. It was outside of a medium size city in the Hudson Valley area. The mental hygiene therapy aides (MHTA's, or TA's for short) had been renamed; instead of attendants; MHTA's was more professional. The TA's would not let him dress the way he wanted to. Ike always liked the lawyers on the TV shows and the suits they wore. He would try to wear his suit every day. Ike only had one suit, for temple, he was told, and the doors to the clothing room were locked because he tried to wear his suit anyway.

Not to mention the other more profoundly ill people that would simply tear clothing to pieces for some unfathomable reason.

This sort of tyrannical treatment continued in his life until one day he moved to Disabled People of America, Inc. and Ferris House. Rosie, his social worker, counseled him that this was his house, along with the other people that live here and that they all had certain rights. Rights to things in the house (within reason) and protection of his and the others' personal property as well as other rights he now possessed.

"Now Ike, you know if I'm in my house I can have anything I want within reason," Rosie kindly told Ike during one session. "This is how you should feel when you move into this new house and live there. And you have a right to your privacy and to your own things."

Ike had been getting used to living like a regular person. He liked to feel as if he lived in a home—his home—with people that he could live with in safety and peace for the first time in his life, like a family, not in fear as he had lived for so long. To be denied this basic right which had finally been given to Ike after over thirty years in an institutional system was too much to tolerate. Ike finally snapped and lost command of his already shredded self control. Righteous indignation took over.

"YOOOOUU," he reacted. He acted the only way he knew how, the same technique he learned to protect himself with at the institution.

"Shit," He bellowed. And used that vulgar language that used to empower him with his mother. **"Shit,"** he repeated with great satisfaction, as he took a lamp and threw it into a wall, ***'CRASH'.*** *That felt good,"* he thought to himself as he basked momentarily in this new found power. He went to pick up another lamp to vent his shame and fury; he grabbed it off the end table, cocked his arm back to give it the old number one into the wall—and was promptly assaulted from behind viciously without warning.

Samantha laced her arm under and around Ike's arm and put him in a half nelson, as though she were some sort of ring-side Rosie. Ike dropped the lamp to the floor, ***'CRASH'.*** His other arm was handled much the same way. Ike was now in a full nelson and was being impelled forward face down onto the couch.

"Now you will have to clean this shit up too," Samantha shouted angrily as she forced him roughly down to the couch.

Ike's face was pressed into the cushions of the couch, he couldn't breathe; he battled frantically for air for a few moments until he became dizzy and stopped the struggle. He lay weakly, immobile, on the couch. Finally Samantha got up and happened to turn to the window where she saw Hector going off outside, witness to the event …

"Get outta' here Hector — go look at your bushes," Samantha bellowed.

Ike only heard this from what seemed like a great distance away as he finally was able to gasp for precious air. She turned back to Ike.

"Now I have to write you up, more **crap-damned** paper work," Samantha screamed, actually frothing at the mouth like a rabid animal. "All you had to do was clean the living room. You shit retard. Once your doctor gets a hold of this behavior you're sure to get more med's. And you need them too."

Samantha was talking more to reassure herself and to catch her breath than for any other reason. As her anger began to abate she saw Ike a little more clearly and became a little nervous with what she saw. He was still gasping for air and looked pale. His lips had a gray/blue color.

"Well if you hadn't a gone off I would not have had to wrap you," she tried to reassure herself with more bluster.

Ike was finally getting his breath back. He was petrified of Samantha but still angry and met her blameful gaze.

"I'm … gonna' tell … Samantha … and you'll be **fired-fired-fired**," Ike wheezed, some of his anger working for him, getting him past his fear and lack of oxygen. Samantha froze. This statement scared her. Not only could she lose her job but she might be brought up on criminal charges.

"Now Ike you don't have to do that," Samantha blurted out. The blush of fear was apparent on her face even to Ike. Trying to control her fear she talked fast. "I'm sorry that happened—that I had to wrap you." In a more accusing tone Samantha tried to get the upper hand back.

"**YOU** should not have broken the lamps. That's going to come out of your bank account."

"My arm hurts," Ike declared as he sat up.

Samantha froze again. "*All I need is another incident report, more paper work, shit,*" she thought. "Look, Ike," Samantha purred in her very best, persuasive fashion.

"Why don't you have that yogurt cup like you wanted and we can be friends again?"

Ike looked up at her, confused at this sudden change in Samantha.

"As a matter of fact have two, we'll celebrate our friendship and I won't even write you up for the lamps, I'll say it was an accident, it was my fault," she finished.

Ike slowly processed this new information. He was feeling better now that he could breathe again and the appeal of food was always a strong enticement.

"Ok Samaaantha," Ike said. But he had wised up since he had been in his new home. He was disabled not stupid. "I waant coookies." Ike smiled to her slyly.

Samantha almost crapped herself at being '*manipulated by a tard'* as she thought of Ike and the other people that live there. But she also knew she was stuck and getting in deeper.

"My arm hurts," Ike said again.

Samantha looked at Ike's arm and there was a large red abrasion on his upper arm where he hit it on the arm of the couch during their little tussle.

"Shit," Samantha muttered under her breath. "Good Ike, cookies it is, you just relax and I'll get us both something, turn on the TV if you want, I'll be right back. Oh yeah Ike if anyone asks just tell them you scraped your arm on the doorway, cause you slipped into it and I'll give you some chocolate milk with your cookies, OK?"

"OK Samantha," Ike said slowly, eyeing her skeptically.

Ike was taken in; he watched as she left the room. He knew He'd won something, but his arm and shoulder still hurt. Ike sat back to wait for his cookies and chocolate milk, he still didn't like the way Samantha treated him but he also wanted the tasty treats. Ike turned on the TV and waited …

Outside Hector heard a commotion from inside his house He bound away from his usual spot near the forsythia over to the living room window. He peered in through the drapes. Hector stood completely still for the count of three, (something he rarely did), then began to jump up and down and slap his head with both hands.

"EEEeee, EEEeee, EEEeee," Hector screamed. Inside he saw Samantha struggling with Ike then throw him down on the couch and hold him down with her considerable mass until Ike's struggles slowed and then stop.

Hector became frantic for Ike's life. He slapped the side of the house beside the window with both hands, frenzied. SLAP, SLAP, SLAP, just as Hector thought his head would burst with frustration—when he could almost feel the distressing inability of Ike's criminal suffocation as though it were his own—suddenly just when Hector thought he couldn't breath anymore himself. Samantha got up off of Ike. He lay there gasping for air. Samantha looked over at the window and into Hector's eyes. The look of maniacal rage directed at Hector jarred him like a physical blow.

"Get outta' here Hector, go look at your bushes," Samantha screamed like a demon from regular person hell. Hector took off as if Samantha were a banshee from some childhood nightmare coming bizarrely through the wall after him. Uncontrollable primal fear in the pit of his belly catapulted him. Within seconds he was back to the imagined safety of his forsythia in the backyard; feeling safer in his bushes. He looked for the auburn haired lady in her garden, and hoping desperately to find some solace. He jumped up and down for some moments slapping his head then he continued his physical triad to gain control over his fear and frustration by rocking back and forth frantically. Soon his emotions were coming under control and he slowly assumed his usual pace. Hector did not forget Samantha's assault on Ike; this went into his considerable pile of tortured memories and abuses that he had seen over the years. To say nothing of the ones he himself had experienced, another nightmare for that dark place on the darkest of nights. Certainly with more to come for Hector.

The van with Shadoe and crew pulled into the parking lot at the humane society. Darla got out of the van first and went over to the van side door, opened it up and took the leash from Chico.

"Now you guys take it easy when we get in here. Don't get all emotional on me," Darla warned.

Sally looked at her with intense concern in her eyes.

Chico faced her intently, a stalwart.

"Ok Darla, we'll be good," Chico courageously stated in the short chopped mode of speech he sometime used when he was tense with, but also reconciled to, an impending fate.

They proceed into the office. There a middle-aged woman with short blond hair along with a 'cutie-pie' teen-age young lady with bi-color hair, obviously her assistant, were simultaneously talking on the phone and conversing with people standing at the counter. Darla eyeballed the older woman on the phone who smiled at her and held up her index finger.

The gang patiently waited several minutes. Momentarily Shadoe started to curiously sniff around on the floor with her tail between her legs. Some of the occupants from Ferris House also began to wander around. Intrigued by the barking of dogs on the other side of a door at one end of the reception room Sally came over to Darla excited.

"Can we take another dog home to keep Shadoe company?" she inquired eagerly.

Chico and Mark both turned and look at Darla in anticipation.

Darla tried to refocus them. "We don't know if we are going to keep this one yet, so don't push your luck."

They all backed off, not wanting to jinx Shadoe's potential adoption. Finally the blond haired woman hung up the phone.

"Can I help you?" she looked quizzically at Darla and the gang.

Darla smiled her best (let's be pals) smile. "Yes, I called before about the stray…"

"Are you Darla Johnson?" the woman asked.

"That's right," Darla affirmed.

The blond haired woman glanced over at the group and smiled kindly at everyone as she pulled a form out and handed it to Darla. "Could you please fill this out?"

Meanwhile, Clark, Sally and Chico were talking to Shadoe and petting her. After several minutes Darla gave back the completed form. The blond lady took it and introduced herself.

"My name is Linda, ask for me if you have any questions when you call."

Linda looked down at Shadoe who had a happy dog smile on her face.

"Seems like a real sweetie-pie," she said to Darla.

"Yeah she's a-a-a good dog, we want t-t-t-to keep her," Chico put in. His eyes blink in rhythm with his anxious stutter.

Sally looked on with concern. Clark was profoundly uncomfortable; he looked nervously at the people around him and just as quickly away so he didn't have to make eye contact with anyone.

"We don't know what we are going to do yet Linda. I'm sure you understand. Please tell us what our obligations are before we can claim this dog legally," Darla smiled and gestured around to the group.

Linda went through the litany of obligations which would make it possible to claim the dog.

"OK, thank you," Darla inhaled then slowly exhaled.

Linda looked at everyone slowly with that same gentle benevolent look that she probably used on everyone who came through the door, human or animal. She was one of those people that made it all worthwhile. Then she came out from around the counter and gently asked Sally for the leash. Sally was overwhelmed with trepidation. She looked wretchedly at Linda.

"You won't … hurt … her?" Sally's eyes began to grow moist.

The others looked on with apprehension, afraid to even breathe. Linda tenderly and effortlessly smiled at Sally.

"Don't worry honey," Linda began. "I'll take care of her as though she were my own. If you guys decide you can have her, if the owners don't come for her, she'll be waiting here for you and I will personally keep an eye on her. And while we go through the process you guys can come and visit her as things are being worked out."

Sally looked into Linda's kindly eyes for a long beat then suddenly decided that it was OK to give over the leash. Ike and Chico simply looked on not knowing what to do as they had never been in a situation like this one before. As Linda took the leash, Darla broke the spell.

"OK you guys, let's go home. We obviously have a lot to talk about. We have to tell Ike and Hector what happened here and we have to plan to see what will happen if we can keep her. BUT most importantly, if we can't keep her we have to be able to handle that too. Does everyone understand what I said?" No one says anything at first. "Well?" Darla prompted. Sally? Clark? Chico? Abigail?"

Abigail did a few bars of one of her indiscriminate tunes, low almost under her breath.

"You guys have to know that we will not be able to keep her if she has a good home. And the agency has to approve her if we can keep her," Darla finished.

They were silent, everyone proceeded out to the van. Once all were inside and belted in, Darla started the engine.

"You guys know we have to have a house meeting today to straighten all this out," she reiterated.

The group grumbled in a low noncommittal tone, barely agreeing as they pulled out of the parking lot onto the main road.

5
The Next Step

(It's a Doozy)

Hector was over by the property line rocking and tapping his chest with his right hand. He looked over into the next yard where the lady with blue eyes played with her plants. He felt good and content with the smells of spring and all the green around him. He was on an even keel once again.

He thought of the dog that had been playing with his roommate Chico. He felt the air of happiness and contentment from Chico and also how the dog felt as they played chase the stick. He also thought of the horrific abuse that he saw applied to Ike and for a moment started to slap his head viciously and jump up and down once more. He contemplated the blue eyed lady again and the inspiration of her beauty. Watching her work on her rose garden always soothed him a little; he stopped hitting himself in frustration but began to rock back and forth ferociously.

The blue eyed lady with whom he was infatuated was not working in her garden as of yet. He missed her when she was not there. For some reason he could feel a profound feeling of peace and contentment radiate from her when she worked in her garden; even more so when the tall man that lived with her came over to her and he could feel the devotion linking them, see a comfortable dedication that flowed between them.

He was not jealous of this, nor envious; he instinctively knew that this was a good thing, something that he would like to, and sometimes did feel about some of the others around him. He saw movement in the window of her house facing him and wished he could go over as a regular neighbor might, but he felt barred by his learned self-deprecation. Taught to him from a cruel system created by blind ignorance. Trapped on this spot Hector simply continued to rock back and forth, watching.

Next door in the kitchen of Marc and Joan Ferris, Joan had fed Marc lunch; she bade him farewell as he went out to the pole barn to take another tractor load of vegetables to the roadside stand, where Martha, a young local woman, would sell them to the summer people.

There were a lot of seasonal people that came to the area, as there existed many little nooks and crannies near the woods and local lakes that drew the elites up to the 'sticks' for their imagined escape.

She looked out of her kitchen window past her garden and through the dense shrubbery bordering their property. She gazed at her brother-in-law's old house, which he had sold to Disabled People of America, Inc. The retard house, as some of her neighbors despicably still called it and probably always would. She saw the tall lanky Asian fellow violently rocking back and forth as he slapped his head in obvious distress. She wanted to speak to him but the last time she tried she spooked him and he ran like a wild mustang. So she simply watched him quietly through her kitchen window. She was torn with the desire of how or if she could console him from whatever unknown pain, emotional or otherwise, that afflicted him. She could easily distinguish the terrible distress he was experiencing by his fervent activity.

This was the type of person Joan was. If she saw someone in physical pain or obvious suffering, her first impulse was to help. As she studied Hector, he eventually began to calm down and assume the typical behavior to which Joan had become accustomed to seeing from him.

Joan reflected on what could have gotten the man so highly agitated, on what he may perhaps be thinking. She eventually realized if she could reason that problem out, she could also probably pick the winning lottery numbers for the next drawing. Suddenly, she saw the van pull into his driveway; Hector dashed from his position near the property line and sprinted to the edge of the driveway where in moments the van would park. By the time the van pulled up, he was standing there as though he hadn't left that spot for two hours.

Darla proceeded down the driveway to park the van in its usual spot and saw Hector standing there, rocking as though he was slightly agitated. She had become used to slight variations in his behavior as well as the others in the house. A sort of an early warning system if she paid attention closely enough.

"Look, there's Hector; he waited for us," Chico said.

"So he did," Darla muttered. *"I wonder if something happened to make Hector anxious while we were away."*

As she contemplated this thought She moved on to the chore of getting everyone into the house from the van and filling the others in on what happened with Shadoe, as at least some of them were dying to know.

Nunzia, a tall lean local forty something country woman with salt and pepper hair and a cowboy hat, had come in early for the swing shift; she addressed Darla before she could even get into the door.

"So what's this I hear about a mutt?" Nunzia rolled her eyes and smirked.

Nunzia was the type of person that knew how everyone should live their lives better than they did. She also had the talent of getting people to like her because she could now and again be charming.

"Oh, she's no mutt, she's adorable and she's probably smarter than you, Nunzia," Darla smiled, taking up the challenge forthwith.

Nunzia smirked again and stuck her tongue out at Darla. Just then Ike walked into the house, and stuck his tongue out at Nunzia, gave a little laugh and declared.

"Nunzia's heeeerrrrreeee," and he laughed again.

"Hiii Ike," Nunzia smiled in a slightly impudent spurious fashion that Ike of course did not pick up, but this did extract a warning glare from Darla. Nunzia just opened her eyes innocent wide and smart-ass smiled off toward Darla. She then started in with some 'alleged' sage advice.

"It's a good thing you took that stray where it should be, the pound. In 30 days you won't have to worry about it anymore anyway," she said.

Sally walked in having only caught the last part of the conversation.

"It will take 30 days for us to get Shadoe back?" Sally asked slowly in a concerned perplexed manner.

Nunzia smirked again at Darla and walked out of the kitchen leaving her with Sally's concerned look.

Darla was deeply moved by Sally's question. She shot a look of steel at Nunzia's back as she exited the room and then turned to Sally.

"Sally, sweetheart, we have to have a house meeting before we can see what everyone wants to do about Shadoe; there are a lot of possibilities we have to talk about, ok sweetie?" Darla smiled.

Sally smiled at Darla. Trusting Darla's word, Sally then continued on with her business of doing those things she did when she was at home.

After dropping off Shadoe, Sally still had Saturday chores to do when she got back home. Sally went up to her room and automatically began to pick up what little clutter was still there; most of it was over by Abigail's part of the room. She just put Abigail's things on her bed. Sally knew it was not right to Abigail's things but she had O.C.D. (obsessive compulsive disorder) and was driven to do more, although with medication it was mostly under control, hardly ever noticeable.

While she worked she thought back to the time in her life before she came to Ferris House. As Sally thought back to her earlier existence she did not realize how wealthy her family was. Her nanny had tried to teach her many things from a young age. Although her nanny, Sara, knew that Sally was a little 'slower' than some of the other children she had worked with over the years, she applied the same dogged determination as she had with all the children she assisted throughout her decades as a nanny. Because of this attention at an early age, although Sally was retarded she possessed a wide array of experiences that helped pattern her into the well rounded person she had become. By the time she was placed in Ferris House she was an insightful and compassionate individual who happened also to be afflicted with a disability or two.

Sally's mother was a very loving person. When Sally was born she seemed just as normal as any other child. As her first year passed it became obvious to her mother that Sally's progress was average at best. Then it became more obvious that her progress as well as development was much less than average. She was exhibiting symptoms of some mental deficiency.

Sally would be caught in a family social situation she had no power over and could not understand.

Sally's father, Jonathan R. Stanton, was a very successful lobbyist at the Capitol. Of course he had her taken to the best experts in the country to evaluate the problem. Unmistakably, the diagnosis was found to be mild mental retardation. Mr. Stanton, although technically a wiz at his profession, did not seem to have enough ingenuity left over for Sally; he could not possibly have a substandard child, he thought. Of course it was easy with his other two children, Jonathan Jr. and Suzanne, as they were over-achievers at a young age. So he didn't give the same attention to Sally, as it was easier to ignore the concern. Sally was again the one that suffered.

Sally's mother Marilyn, was at least as compassionate as any good mother. She had plenty of love for all her children, Sally included, regardless of any differences. By the time Sally began to reach puberty the shame of having a retarded child simply became too much for Jonathan R. Stanton, Sr. Many evenings after the children had gone to bed, over martinis and white wine, they first discussed, then argued upon the fate of little Sally. Unbeknownst to them, little Sally, although disabled, was a very bright and curious girl and would sneak to the top the steps and eavesdrop on their sometimes over-rambunctious discussions about her future.

Sally knew it was all her fault that she had been born substandard and was fittingly ashamed. So when the day finally came where she was placed on the campus of Disabled People of America, Inc., she knew that this was what she deserved for being Inferior. This statement as per her father, whom she still loved very much to this day despite his frosty attitude toward her.

The adjustment to the atmosphere in which Sally found herself immersed at Disabled People of America's campus was intense. Thank God, Sally was one of those special people whose emotional demeanor was very passionate and forgiving. Couple this with an unstoppable resiliency and intuitiveness and she continued to thrive. She, of course, had the added advantage of being placed at the Disabled People of America's organization, whose people were exceedingly well versed in the understanding that retarded people were merely less-able than the rest of the population. Their philosophy was that everyone had the ability to learn and achieve their best given time and support. And that if you treat people with dignity they would respond in kind.

Sally's mother's methodology was the other oh so crucial element which enabled her to survive that first grueling year. They kept in touch, visited regularly, and Marilyn Stanton had Sally home for all the birthdays, holidays, and any special family events that would take place in the normal course of any family's existence.

The depth of Sally's mother's compassion was such that she did not bring Sally home for any of these family events simply to be vindictive to her husband, who obviously was not gifted with anything near the saintly compassion and understanding of Sally's mother, but out of the genuine kindness and loving understanding that only a compassionate mother could supply. She was able to look past Sally's disabilities to the inner character in her personality, a gift that fortunately made them both so forgiving in the end.

In some ways this benevolence made it even more difficult for her father to cope. Because of Sally's inner generosity and mercy, the same traits derived from her mother. Her father was never openly confronted by either mother or daughter with his inability to face so difficult a circumstance regarding his deficiency. Mother and daughter both dealt with this awkward existence until the mother's death of breast cancer several years into Sally's exile.

This innate ability of exoneration which Sally inherited from her mother always shined through, as her compassionate and generous demeanor was a joy to anyone who took the trouble to get to know her …

Downstairs Darla was talking to Nunzia. "I'm afraid to ask, but did you feed the guys while we went to the animal shelter?"

Nunzia gave that smirking, smart-ass half smile.

"Of course I fed them, it was feeding time at the zoo, wasn't it? The livestock would be bellering a lot louder than they are now if I hadn't," Nunzia articulated. "It was easier to feed these two than try to get Samantha off of the computer," she continued. "Oh and by the by Samantha said she had to leave early because her babysitter called and little Tommy was sick."

“Oh, you are so amusing Nunzia,” Darla answered in a formidably sarcastic tone, but was also happy that she only had one smart ass to deal with for the rest of her afternoon. Nunzia smirked and went into the other room.

Darla went to the refrigerator to see what was left over from lunch. She pulled out a large bowl of recently refrigerated macaroni & cheese, and parked it in the microwave to start to reheat it. She went over to the hallway near the steps and called upstairs.

“Sally, Chico, Mark, Abigail ... come on down and set the table for lunch.”

She heard various calls of assent from upstairs. Darla went back into the kitchen. Minutes later the late lunch eaters converged on the kitchen. In the dining room there were various interactions between them as they went through the usual motions of preparing to eat lunch. Nunzia took the others outside to do more yard work so there were no incidents from having two different lunch shifts in the house.

After lunch, and after more yard work was completed, Ike came in from outside.

“Are we going to go for a ride, Darla?” he asked.

Darla watched as Abigail started the dishwasher. “Aren’t you concerned about Shadoe?”

Ike began to scratch one hand with the other, gave a little smile. “Shaadooe, can we keep her?”

Darla smiled at Ike benignly. “I think it would be a good idea for a little house meeting about Shadoe this afternoon instead of going for a ride. Plus we’re one short since Samantha had to go home.”

At the sound of Samantha’s name, Ike got a funny look on his face for a brief instant and rubbed his upper arm ... Darla studied him for a moment.

“I think you should go ask Nunzia if she wants to participate in the house meeting about Shadoe, Ike you know how Nunzia ‘loves’ house meetings.”

“Ah-ha ha,” Ike gave a little laugh. “Oookaayy Darla.”

Nunzia walked into the room having overheard Darla’s suggestion that Ike seek her out to discuss a house meeting which pertained to Shadoe. She beamed petulant fire from her eyes straight at Darla. Darla returned Nunzia’s burning gaze with a round eyed innocence in her calm brown eyes which served only to exacerbated Nunzia's attitude.

"I think it's time for a meeting, Nunzia; you can take the notes, and if I ever hear you call these people livestock again we will discuss it with Elmer."

The fire drained from Nunzia's eyes and she purred like a kitten. "It would be my pleasure to take notes, Darla, why don't you run and fetch me a pen and paper."

Before Darla could react Nunzia turned on her heels and began to bellow through the house like a town crier.

"House meeting, five minutes in the dining room," she shouted.

A cascade of answers greeted her as she continued her exaggerated role.

Shortly everyone was seated patiently around the dining room table. Darla was officiating the meeting; Nunzia taking notes.

"Ok," Darla began. She looked around at everyone at the table; Clark alternately looked at her, then away as was his habit. Hector was standing, gently rocking.

"Please sit down Hector," she asked.

Hector sat but continued to gently rock back and forth. Abigail was looking at the table jogging one leg in place as she usually did when she was trying to focus on something. Sally smiled joyously as if she already knew they would keep Shadoe. Ike sat like a toad on a log, and Chico looked at Nunzia and as his mouth opened wide with the effort to confront her usual callousness, he got out.

"Nunzia, I-I-I want to keep the dog."

Nunzia smirk/smiles back. "No you don't Chico, think of all the hair you will have to clean up when it's your turn to vacuum the carpets."

Chico's voice gathered some surety and he lost most of his stutter.

"I-I don't care, I like to vacuum," he smiled happily.

Darla abruptly knocked on the table with her knuckles before Nunzia could retort.

"All right, this house meeting of Ferris House comes to order. We are here to discuss Shadoe the dog and see what our options are as the residents of this house," she announced.

Everyone sat still except for Hector who rocked gently in his chair.

"W-w-w-we … w-w-want to keep Shadoe, she's our dog now," Chico stammered out, in his trepidation over the bond he and the others had already built up with the dog.

"It's not that easy," Darla insisted as she ignored a sneering grin from Nunzia. "As the nice lady at the shelter told us, to hold the dog for two weeks to make sure no one claims her; then we can go through the adoption process. But we also have to talk to the bosses at the agency. We have to see if we are allowed to have this dog."

Chico spoke up again. "C-Chucky my friend a-at Shawnee House has a dog, a dog named Salamander."

"Yeah," Sally chimed in, "I seen him, he's one of those hot-dog dogs."

Abigail sat still humming a made up tune of her own, apparently oblivious to what was happening around her.

Clark found his courage, which was rare and looked at Darla. "Dogs are good, I like dogs."

Darla sighed. "I know they have a dog at Shawnee House, and most dogs are good, and I think Shadoe is a good dog before you guys ask," Darla answered. "But let's settle down and take it one step at a time."

Nunzia couldn't help it any longer, she simply had to antagonize, it was a hobby that gave her great pleasure and she was good at it. She taunted the people around the table.

"The little girl that lost that mutt is probably picking her up right now," she stated, smiling evilly.

"Noo," burst out Sally in fear, tears welling up in her innocent eyes.

Clark quickly looked down at his hands in disgrace as if his finally speaking out was somehow related to them not being able to keep Shadoe.

Chico simply looked upset enough to weep along with Sally.

Nunzia grinned gleefully, having had her fun, and after triumphantly surveying her handiwork around the table, looked at Darla, whose eyes were boiling with barely suppressed fury. Nunzia, not easily intimidated, smiled sweetly at Darla. For an instant Darla stared at Nunzia considering if she should say something now or later. She broke the stare being the first to look away, not out of disadvantage, but momentary discretion.

"Not here— not now," she thought to herself. "Now everyone calm down, just settle down," she said.

Everyone started to settle and began to focus back on Darla as she drew their attention away from a malicious Nunzia.

"I will call the main campus on Monday and start the ball rolling," she paused for a moment thoughtfully. "Maybe Nunzia might want to take some of you guys after dinner today or maybe tomorrow to visit with Shadoe and see if you are permitted to walk her," Darla smiled gazing at Nunzia, daring her to react.

Everyone at the table erupted with excitement, even silent Hector smiled and tapped his chest two or three times lightly. Nunzia's face darkened with animosity as she realized that Darla had outwitted her. She will now have to be on her best behavior in public and couldn't have as much fun with everyone's emotions as she may have liked; also she would not be able to escape taking her charges to see the beast.

"Now if there are no more comments or questions … we will follow the plan as we set it down and the meeting will be now adjourned," Darla paused again. She smiled at Nunzia pointedly and everyone around the table more kindly. "Alright let's get everything around here cleaned up and get ready for dinner. I think Abigail and Sally were cooking tonight; Clark and Hector were setting the table. Nunnnzy," Darla purred, "who would you like to help with their dinner chores?"

"You're the boss Darla dear," Nunzia purred right back...

Later, after dinner and the clean up, as everyone was pre-occupied with their various endeavors of relaxation. Abigail, Sally, and Nunzia were sitting in the living room watching TV. Ike and Clark eventually wandered in to see what was on television and ended up mesmerized by the tube along with the others. Hector was in his favorite spot, also in the living room, rocking back and forth in a very relaxed manner.

Chico shyly came up to Darla who was sitting in the office working on someone's records. "D-D-Darla, c-can I e-mail my friend, Chucky at Shawnee house?"

Darla continued to write for a split second more, then closed the binder and looked up.

"Sure, do you know how to open the I.M.?" she asked.

"Yeah!" Chico happily blurted.

He almost knocked Darla over as she moved away from the desk so Chico could take the chair. Darla watched Chico with amusement.

"Just turn off the computer when you're done; it's not good to leave it on all night and I might forget too, ok?" she asked.

Chico was already logging on to the I.M. It had taken some time for Elmer and others at the house to teach Chico to I.M. to the other houses. It was a program set up to teach the people they served to try to do more for themselves, as well as help them to be more a part of society at large.

Chico got logged on and took sometime to compose his first message.

"Hi chuky this is chico are you hom?" *Enter.*

A few minutes later a message came back from Chucky.

"I saw you on thescreen caus I was there hi."

Chico took a few minutes to read the message then five or six more minutes to compose one.

"We hav a new dog we fond today we did n t go to bowlin." *Enter.*

After another five or six minutes Chucky's IM came back.

"We hav a dog to we went to se movie today but i want to com overto see you new dog."

After puzzling through this message Chico prepared the next message and sent it.

After almost two hours of IMing and a shift change, the night shift came to work and began 'relaxing' for the night after doing a minimum of necessary overnight duties, and after telling Chico not to be too long on the computer. Chico finally logged off, rubbing his eyes with weary abandon.

Hector was in the office with Chico gently rocking back and forth. Almost from the start Hector had been in the same spot while Chico had his session with Chucky. They could hear the television in the living room as the night shift had long ago congregated there to watch late night repeats as they tried to doze, hoping for a quiet night. The evening shift had long since gone home and the rest of the people in the house were performing their nocturnal activities of sleeping, watching TV in their rooms, or whatever.

Chico again rubbed his eyes and got tiredly up from the computer.

"Come on Hector let's go to bed I'm tired."

He went to leave the room and when Hector didn't follow; he tried to take Hector's hand and lead him as he knew this sometimes worked. Hector pulled away and slapped his head once or twice making a loud noise.

"Don't do that, you will get the nightshift mad at us," Chico whispered.

Chico, not wanting to get into trouble, waved both hands at Hector in a pushing away motion.

"Suit yourself," he said.

A phrase he had heard attendants say to him over the years when he was being stubborn about something.

"I'm going to bed; stay up all night if you have to."

Chico left the room, turning off the light, hoping to influence Hector and went upstairs.

Once again, Hector moved over in front of the computer and stared at the monitor. He stared and continued to rock back and forth in a very relaxed fashion —seemingly in a trance. He watched the screen-saver, set on the star field. As the stars zoomed past him, he keened quietly with delight …

6
Fun in the Community (If this is fun shoot me now)

The next day was of course Sunday morning. Once again the members of the household had to contend with their psychotropic drug-induced hangover.

The nightshift people were also contending with either sleep deprivation, if they were the type to stay up all night as required by agency policy, or like many, made themselves at home and slept as soon as the rest of the house was out cold. Possibly some of them could even sleep through an earthquake. In any case the residents of Ferris House were slowly waking up to a quiet Sunday morning, or at least quiet so far, but it was early.

As morning medications were passed out, the residents straggled into the kitchen looking for breakfast. Some of the inhabitants fought with their fuzzy-brain as they tried to make some sort of breakfast. Others succumbed to the chemical influence and simply rolled over for more shut-eye. Darla, on the schedule this morning, was tired from having to work an evening shift the night before and then having to come in for the early shift. Samantha was passing med's while Darla assisted people with their various undertakings of culinary fare.

"Samantha, isn't Ike up yet? He always gets up for his Sunday morning pancakes even after a behavior like he had yesterday," Darla inquired.

"I have to give him his med's anyway, Darla, I'll see if he's ok," Samantha casually remarked.

Samantha inwardly cringed as she went into Ike's room; Ike was still in bed lying on his back with his covers pulled up to his nose. His eyes followed Samantha's every move apprehensively. As inoffensively as she was able Samantha cooed.

"Come on Ike it's time to rise and shine, Aren't you hungry?"

Ike just stared at her for a moment like a dog that had been kicked too many times.

"Come on, Darla is waiting to make you pancakes with blueberries, your favorite. Also I want you to take your med's," she finished.

Ike from under his covers finally reacted. "Fuck you Samaaanthaa." He looked for a reaction to his vulgarity.

"Now that's no way to speak to someone. You don't want to be written up for another behavior do you?"

Samantha tried to verbally intimidate Ike into her control. No reaction. "You know this already looks bad after yesterday's outburst."

Ike tried to think; the Phenobarbital he was on to control his seizures kept him somewhat dopey. Ike dazedly tried to remember the events of yesterday morning but it was coming back slowly. Samantha kept interrupting his concentration.

"Look Ike, I'll tell Darla that you said you will be out in a little while. When you do come out, stop and get your med's on the way to the kitchen. Ok? Ok," Samantha finished then made tracks.

Ike got doggedly back to his thoughts of yesterday. He knew he was angry at Samantha for hurting him. All he wanted was a snack like he saw regular people get. Like Rosie his social worker told him (anything within reason). Ike struggled out of bed and prepared to get dressed for the day, thinking of his Sunday morning pancakes and Darla. His friend Darla, who always helped him with making pancakes when she was there.

Out in the kitchen Darla looked at Samantha quizzically.

"So is Ike coming out?"

Nonchalantly, Samantha sat down at the large dining room table amid the others having breakfast. She started to go over her paper work.

"He said he would be out in a little while. You know him; he doesn't want to miss making breakfast with his pal Darla."

Darla studied Samantha's back from the kitchen a for moment; she knew it was in bad taste to talk about the residents with others around but did anyway.

"So it's been some time since Ike had a rough morning like yesterday huh?" Darla tested the waters.

An almost unnoticeable tension passes across Samantha's shoulders then was gone.

"Yeah, but who knows what set him off, he knows he can't use violent behavior to get what he wants, all he has to do was ask. I would have been happy to help him with whatever he needed. I think he is targeting me because I don't cater to him like some others do around here."

Samantha stopped writing and had even put down her pen. She calmly went through her proclamation her back to Darla. Almost as if her statement were rehearsed from a script.

Hector was rocking at the table as he finished his food and began to rock harder as the tension mounted in the room between Darla and Samantha. Sally and Abigail were just settling into their places with their plates of food which Darla had assisted them in preparing. At this point Darla felt sure something possibly bad had transpired more than the incident report claimed.

"That's funny," Darla began. "I've known Ike a long time and usually it takes something to—"

Just then Ike lumbered into the kitchen. Darla watched how Ike seemed tense as he went around the table the long way seemingly to avoid Samantha.

"Hi Ike, how are you this morning?" Samantha asked in a jubilant but controlled tone, feigning joy in seeing him.

Darla on the other hand, was genuinely happy to see Ike. She was one of those gifted people who receive great joy working with people less able. For her it was more than a job, it was a calling. Ike sensed this in Darla as did all the others around the table. This relaxed him right away.

"Hiii Daarla," Ike smiled.

"Good morning Ike, how are you today?" Darla literally sang back to Ike. "Are you hungry?"

"Pancakes Darla," Ike blurted out happily.

"That's what I figured, come over and I will help you make some breakfast."

As Ferris House was stirring from slumber, concurrently there was activity at 348 Ferris Road. Joan and Marc being raised country folk were early birds. Five o'clockers they were, already finished with breakfast and outside on the go so as not to waste the day.

Marc was doing those things necessary to get the vegetable stand ready for the seasonal people, as well as the neighbors that simply like to eat fresh vegetables instead of frozen or canned.

Joan was as usual in her favorite rose garden spreading mulch around her roses. She again developed that feeling as though she was being watched. She looked up to see if her elusive friend was watching, as he usually was. This did not bother her. She was a great believer in perceptions and had strong intuition.

In the short time that Hector lived next door and had scrutinized her she had only sensed peaceful feelings about him. She saw his figure partially hidden again behind the forsythia at the edge of the property and recognized Hector's familiar shape and his gentle rocking back and forth movement.

She patiently worked in her garden for a brief while then came to a command decision. "*Maybe I'll try to talk to him again, it's the Christian thing to do and it is the Lords day.*" She took the plunge and tiptoed a little closer so she didn't have to shout and possibly startle him.

"Hello? Hello?" She took a step closer. The figure moved concealing itself deeper into the forsythia, same as the last time.

There was still a bit of shade, an early morning gloom … the sun was not yet over the hill, a residue of nighttime moisture off the trees and other vegetation had left a slight mist close to the the ground in a few low spots. It was almost like one of those old horror movies. In the obscurity, the at-first outwardly benign figure had frozen almost ominously, again still as stone. Now Joan stopped. She suddenly had a different feeling, unlike the one she usually had when she looked at her resident prowler. For the first time since he had been watching her she astonishingly was on the defensive. For Joan, a formidable personality, this felt peculiar. Joan shook this notion off, feeling foolish. The typical Joan took charge.

"Can I help you?" Joan stated in a friendly but firm voice.

She began to feel a little better; a cloud moved over the rising of the morning sun which had begun to dispel some of the early morning murk, again casting the intruder back into the shadows. He took a step out into the open. Joan stopped cold and saw him in all his apparent emaciated glory. Hector, she knew, merely lived next door, just one of her new neighbors.

But she sensed an ability of understanding in him, an oddly almost inherent astuteness as he regarded her.

"Hello," Joan ventured gently.

She spoke as she would in the midst of a frightened child, she quickly regained all of her confidence.

"And what's your name," she inquired.

The lean Asian man stared back at her as a statue might —unmoving. She took a chance and took another step toward him.

"My name is Joan …"

He had not moved at all during this exchange, not committing to either fight or flight.

"And yours is???" she inquired again.

Then in a snap—faster than the speed of light, old E=mc2, before she could even blink, he took off and ran like a young buck with a hunter on his ass out of sight through the adjoining property and disappeared into the back door, same as last time.

"Oh well," Joan whispered to herself. "I guess he's still a little shy."

She turned back to her tranquil pleasure. She loosened up some dirt around a rosebush as she let her memory drift back to earlier days when she and Marc were young and just starting out.

They both had jobs working for the state. The year was 1959; she was a switchboard operator at the local state hospital. Not that she was unapproachable, she was just choosy when it came to men. At the age of 20 years old Joan had a lot going for her. She was a strikingly beautiful woman with auburn hair, light blue eyes and the hourglass shape that was in preference at the time. She also had no end to potential suitors since she came from local money.

When Joan first met Marc he had just transferred to the main building to work in admissions. Marc walked in one morning shortly after she started work for the day and for Joan the chemistry happened as soon as she saw him.

He was a good-looking rugged type about six feet tall with the broad strong shoulders of a man that was not afraid of hard work. He had black hair and those dark eyes that a woman could get lost staring into. Marc was with Harry Thompson, the fellow who told him to take a state job a year earlier.

"Hello Harry, who's the new guy?" Joan asked trying to be friendly.

Harry began to speak but Marc interrupted him.

"I'm Marc Ferris, that's Marc with-a-c."

Although he was trying to be clever, as he thought Joan was very attractive, Joan took it wrong, his seemingly flippant attitude ruffled her feathers —rubbed her the wrong way.

She knew of his family, local farmers, and being a confident individual she lashed out immediately.

"Forget I asked Marc with-a-c."

"That's right you did ask," Marc retorted just as quickly, not wanting to be thought of as a jellyfish.

Marc couldn't believe how bitchy her attitude was and right away wished for a way out. She was pretty and he didn't quite understand how he had offended her but he didn't want her to get the best of him either. Young male ego, don't you know. He stood his ground and waited for her retort which he was not quite ready to receive anyway.

"Hopefully that's the biggest mistake I make today," Joan uttered sardonically.

She turned to the switchboard automatically to handle business.

Marc raised his left hand and gave her a smart-ass salute. Instantly the uncomfortable tension in the air swelled to alarming proportions. Joan gave him a steely-blue-fired glance like a death ray as he walked passed with a smirk on his face.

Down the hall, Harry looked at Marc with apprehension.

"That's the wrong woman to get upset around here. Don't you know who she is?"

Marc seemed a little uncomfortable at the subtle ferocity of his exchange with Joan.

"I don't care who she is, I already know she's a bitch and that only took two seconds. I think I'm in love," Marc declared cynically.

"Suit yourself," Harry muttered as he shoved the key in the lock to Ward Two. "But she comes from big local money and you should be more careful."

Harry dubiously pushed open the door; he and Marc exchanged an ooh-well glance and proceeded to the day's work.

Joan threw a little fertilizer around the loose dirt near her rosebush and started mixing it in, deeply entranced in this memory. Suddenly a hand touched her shoulder. She jumped and twisted around with her shovel at the ready.

"Easy there young lady, a little jumpy today aren't you?"

The smiling face of Marc, her loving husband, mocked her.

"You were an asshole when I met you and you're still an asshole, Marc with-a-c," she said with slight agitation and playfulness in her tone. "I thought you were that fellow from next door again," Joan supposed out loud.

"Oh, was that Chincky kid lurking around again?" Marc looked over to the property line.

"Now Marc that's not proper, I don't call you a Jonny Bull."

"Alright, alright, that or-ie-n-tal fella, was he here again?"

Joan looked off at the trees with a somber look on her face ignoring Marc's jibe.

"Yes he was here again, dear. I had that heebie-jeebies feeling come over me— you know, then I looked up there he was watching me again. That's why I was so jumpy."

Marc had a stern, troubled look on his face. "I'll go over and talk to them. Get them to stay on their own damn property."

"No, no," Joan said hurriedly. "No harm done. He was just curious … like a child."

The troubled look on Marc's face only deepened. "Don't make the mistake of thinking of these people as children; you've been around them long enough to know how unpredictable they can be."

Joan put her left hand on his shoulder and stroked his left jaw line with her index finger, stopping at his chin. "Please honey, it's really no trouble. He really doesn't mean any harm. I'm sure you don't have to protect me from a poor retarded fellow."

The look on Marc's face softened. "Yeah, I guess they don't mean any harm, maybe we should have them over for dinner," Marc said jokingly.

"Now that's a good idea," Joan smiled earnestly.

"NO," barked Marc quickly. "It was a joke."

Then he looked at her with a gleam in his eye, grabbed her chin with his large thumb and forefinger. “You always have to have your way don’t you,” he said with a smile.

“Well Marc with-a-c, I know you’ll want your way with me, so I get to have my way with you,” she smiled seductively.

She pecked him on the lips, and then shut him down quick when his blood started to rise. In a stern voice, Joan suggested.

“Now you have to finish that field so we can get those vegetables in the stand and make our extra vacation money.”

He paused, his shoulders drooped in mock resignation as he turned towards his tractor, then he turned back again to Joan.

“Oh yeah, I almost forgot, I saw Harry Thompson when I was getting parts for the tractor. He and Emma want to know if we want to come over for dinner during the week, they have to clean the venison out of their freezer. The way he hunts I don’t expect that will take long.”

Joan laughed lightheartedly. “And the way she cooks, I imagine that’s why it took so long already.”

They both laughed mischievously.

“I can tell them we’ve got somewhere else to be if you want to get out of it,” Marc said.

“No, no,” pondered Joan, “They’re good people; we don’t want to hurt their feelings.”

“Ok, I’ll call them and let them know we’ll be there Thursday night if that’s good for them,” Marc finished.

Marc turned and walked away. “She wasn’t that polite when I first met her—must be old age,” he muttered under his breath.

As he walked off towards his tractor; Joan went back to her garden and resumed her mulching. She drifted back to her familiar reflections...

Upstairs at Ferris House, Hector looked out of his bedroom window toward the neighboring house and his auburn-haired infatuation. As he rocked back and forth vigorously and slapped his chest, he was watching Joan and Marc through the pane of thermo glass.

Chico walked in and saw Hector was bothered by something. He had learned that when Hector was getting like this it was sometimes good to distract him.

"Come on Hector we have to clean our room or Samantha said I can't go bowling."

Hector jumped up and down and slapped his head. Slap, slap, slap. "EEEeee, EEEeee, EEEeeeeee."

"Come on Hector, I'm your roommate, you have to listen to me."

Chico said this to Hector when he didn't know what to do. He did not want to incur the wrath of Samantha; this thought made him nervous. He gave a quick glance toward the top of the steps to make sure that they were not already discovered, then went over and put his hand on Hector's arm. Hector stopped slapping his head but continued to rock.

"Come on Hector," Chico said, in a more conspiratorial tone. "I-I-I'll help you make your bed, Samantha said I should. She said she has to have her cigarette. Then she said we can have onions on our cheeseburgers when we go bowling, and I'm hungry."

Hector allowed himself to be guided over to his bed by Chico. Chico left Hector at his bedside and proceeded over to his own bed. Hector haphazardly began to pull sheet and covers from the bottom of his bed up to the pillow and stood there rocking, watching Chico as he made his own bed. Chico finished his bed, walked over to Hector and looked up at him. Hector was a good two feet taller than Chico.

"Samantha won't like that bed like that, Hector, she will holler at us again."

Chico neatened it up a little bit. All of a sudden they heard Samantha from downstairs.

"C'mon you guys," Samantha hollered in a bored tone.

"What are you doing up there, those beds better be neat, I'll check." Chico knew by now this was an empty threat because Samantha did not like to get out from in front of the computer. And if she could help it she didn't like to come up the steps, because she was lazy. This is what Chico had heard other staff in the house say of Samantha. In the past her actions had born out this supposition.

"Ok," Chico called down the steps to Sam, "we're done."

"I'm gonna check on it," Samantha retorted threateningly.

Chico mimicked here under his breath. "I'm gonna check on it," Chico muttered, and then nervously restated. "I-I-I know Samantha, we're done, the beds are neat."

From the bottom of the steps Samantha bellowed, "Alright come on down."

She has no real volume control on her voice when she was talking to '*the people that ride the tard cart,*' as she considered the people she served.

"And get ready to go bowling," she finished.

She toddled away toward the office and the computer, her beloved realm.

Upstairs, Chico took Hector's hand. "Come on, Hector, let's go."

They had been roommates since moving into the house. They used to live together in Stanton Hall on the main campus before they moved to Ferris House, but that was with 30 other consumers. They had known each other for sometime. However in the short time they'd been roommates at Ferris House they had developed a workable and in some ways an incredible friendship.

They proceeded down the steps and into the kitchen where Antwan, (another staff member recently transferred to Ferris), endeavored to get Abigail and Sally out of the door and into the van.

Abigail, a 4' 8" woman of 39 years was allowing herself to be led as she hummed an abstract tune. She began to lag behind and drift into another room to sit down.

"You don't have to go bowling if you don't want to," Samantha threatened from the office door.

Abigail stopped humming and quietly got out of her chair and walked to the door followed by an already cowed Sally. Chico watched this exchange.

"I helped Hector with his bed," Chico ventured to say to Samantha.

Samantha ignored Chico's statement and spoke to Antwan as though no one else was in the room. Antwan looked over at Chico and Hector as they stood in the entrance way to the kitchen and winked at them. Hector went into the other room as was his whim and started to rock gently back and forth while he looked out the window toward Joan's house.

Samantha's corpulent jowls quivered as she recited her litany.

"They owe me time or money, they said they'd pay me overtime, but they can't pay me overtime because I had a holiday last week."

Antwan, a six foot five, 220 pound, African American man was as gentle as he was buff. And it could also be said that he had been around the horn, so to speak.

He grabbed a clipboard from of the counter with keys on it and inattentively turned his back on Samantha as she droned on. Clark had joined Chico and they were waiting patiently. Antwan waved the guys toward the door with his eyes rolling, silently mimicking Samantha. Then he acknowledged Samantha's rant.

"They have to do something, Sam," Antwan stated bored. Antwan was a bit impatient as it became even more obvious that he really didn't want to hear Samantha's perpetual complaining.

Samantha waddled toward the office where her beloved computer was. Her voice trailed off.

"I don't know how they can promise me that when they know I had a holiday last week," she faded away.

Antwan looked at Clark and Chico as they passed.

"Are your beds made, guys?"

Chico stopped the procession and looked at Antwan, smiling at Antwan's antics … and again patiently stated as though he were talking to someone who was slow.

"I helped Hector make his bed," Chico repeated again.

Chico had become used to regulars asking the same questions of him over and over and had learned that he had to repeat himself often.

"I made mine too," Clark chimed in. He also was chuckling at Antwan's imitation of Samantha.

"Well that's good enough for me. You guys ready to go? I can use a cheeseburger at the bowling alley snack bar as much as I know you guys can," Antwan said.

Chico smiled and looked all the way up to Antwan. "Me too pal," he answered happily.

Clark and Chico proceeded past Antwan out the door.

"We're leaving now, you need anything?" Antwan called to Samantha in the office.

Samantha popped her head out of the office. "Garbage bags and toilet paper, always pick up garbage bags and toilet paper when you're out. Ok?"

"Ok," Antwan grumbled as he proceeded out the door. "Some women are easy to please, but she ain't one of them," he mumbled to himself.

They all trooped out to the van, loaded up and headed out.

Back inside Samantha lumbered over to the computer in the office. She pulled out her Dunkin Donuts and coffee-mocha-latte-supreme and set it in front of her. She brought up the site she was on before being so rudely interrupted by actually having to work.

"Damned tar tars," she mumbled.

She started to surf the web. First she went to her mailbox to check for the new recipes she had sent to a food site for. She spent a good fifteen minutes reading through them and then e-mailed them to her home computer.

For someone like Samantha food actually had a strong sexual component. She was one of these people who actually got excited when details of a particularly luscious menu were being discussed. Imagining each dish, how its loving-meticulous preparation unfolded. Meat seasoned just right or better yet marinated over a 24 or 48 hour period —how it was cooked over an open flame, slooowwly, to bring out the perfect flavor and seal in succulent, natural juices. How the side dishes were prepared and matched up with the meat. Rich, creamy, luscious, sauces over the vegetables, little roasted potatoes with real butter, homemade bread still hot from the oven with real fresh made preserves.

She was the type of person that essentially had sacrificed the tactile pleasures of human contact for culinary delights. Someone that was emotionally more attached to a roasted leg of lamb sometimes than her own child.

Samantha had even punished her son for not bringing home the proper array of flavors from the store as she sat in front of her computer at home while she sent him out to pick up more food.

While she was so engrossed in this scrumptious tryst on the agency computer, Hector wandered into the office without her knowledge. He had been quietly rocking back and forth in his favorite spot behind her and watched her every move on the

All of a sudden he started to lightly tap his chest while he rocked back and forth as he was apt to do when he was relaxed and enjoying something. Very few know what these enjoyments might be, these things that pleased Hector. But this action of chest tapping was what someone who observed Hector for any length of time saw him perform when he was content. The first tap startled Samantha as she was in her own trance. She jumped out of her skin and turned around with surprising speed and dexterity for someone so large.

"What the Hell …???? Hector you asshole."

This action in turn jolted Hector who started to jump up and down slapping his head while he keened like an abused puppy.

"EEEEEEEE … EEEEEEEEEE!"

"Shut up and get out of here," Samantha screamed.

She lumbered out from behind the desk and chair and charged Hector. Her hands were out to grab him so she could bum-rush him out of the office.

She was like a person that was interrupted just before the point of orgasm—livid with anger and frustration—like a rogue elephant in musk she bore down on Hector and gained momentum. Hector tried to turn and run like the frightened gazelle he had temporarily become, but his typically instantaneous reflexes failed him this rare time. Samantha grabbed him by the belt with both hands one on either side of his waist and propelled him through the open office door with tremendous force.

Samantha's assault coupled with his already building escape velocity propelled Hector like a rocket. He flew face first into the hallway wall and dented the sheetrock with his head.

"Get out of here you skinny little asshole, if you ever do that to me again I'll kill you, you fuckin' retard," screamed Samantha the tormentor.

Hector recovered in a snap and jetted out of the back door high-tailing it to his one safe place of refuge, the shrubs at the border of the auburn haired lady's yard, his palace of solitude.

"Asshole," Samantha spit vehemently.

She was literally shaking with anger and sweating with frustrated rage …

"Asshole," she repeated again to no one in particular. "Screw this, I try to relax a little and with these people I never can."

With not another thought of Hector she went back to the computer and tried to recapture her mood. Finding herself still too overwrought to go on she decided to go to the kitchen to get a little snack. "That'll make me feel better," she thought to herself as she proceeded out of the office …

As Hector was up at his private retreat utilizing the same type coping skills he used at program to settle down... Antwan lumbered into the bowling alley with Chico, Clark, Sally, and Abigail… they trailed behind him like a loose gaggle of ugly ducklings. They proceeded up to the counter amid the usual impolite and sterile stares from inconsiderate, or just curious, or simply bored people, and settled at the service counter on either side of Antwan like a gentle wave.

Marisa, the appealing young woman at the counter, was familiar with everyone in the group and she smiled as she came over to the assemblage.

"So, Antwan, how's it going today?" she oozed. She leaned suggestively over the counter and gave Antwan a predatory grin. "Do you want the usual for them?"

Clark glanced at her ample cleavage and quickly looked away. He found that his eyes were drawn back and he quickly looked away again.

"Why don't you ask them? They can talk," Antwan calmly stated.

"When are you going to take me out again Antwan?" A smiling Marisa ignored Antwan's declaration.

Chico nudged Antwan and smiled up to him. Antwan ignored Chico (who momentarily wandered his gaze to other events going on around him), and tried to get back to business.

"Yes Marisa," Antwan uttered patiently. "You know the sizes everyone needs, get us the shoes and we'll talk later."

Marisa became teasingly business like. "Well who needs what?" she asked.

They all started to talk at once.

"Now one at a time," Antwan cut in.

"Ladies first," Marisa declared, kindly but teasingly reproaching the men.

Abigail looked at Sally; Sally nudged her with her arm and gestured with her head towards Marisa.

"Six," Abigail muttered.

Marisa gave her a size eight, remembering the last time she accidentally contradicted Abigail about her shoe size and the almost outburst that Antwan had to quell with his wit.

This was why Marisa liked Antwan; because he was quick thinking and buff. *"Not just looks,"* Marisa thought to herself.

Sally in a pleasant tone, spoke up next. "Hi Marisa how are you today?"

Genuinely, Marisa gave Sally a big smile. "I'm good sweetie, how are you?"

"OK dear, I'll have a size nine," Sally answered casually.

As this process continued, across the bowling alley there sat a man already on his third beer of the day; Klupkick sat with his equally repulsive drinking buddy, Seymour. Looking daggers at the group, he opened the conversation with the inevitable statement.

"Look at those damned retards. They have a lot a gall bringing them to the bowling alley, how would they like it if I hung out around their house all the time?"

"You drive past it at least three times a day," Seymour volunteered.

"Shut up Seymour, I didn't ask you. It ain't like they can bowl like normal people," Klupkick groused. He took another manly gulp of his cheap domestic beer. His drinking buddy Seymour piped up again to add more of his infinite wisdom into the mix.

"The one ain't too bad lookin' for a retard girl," Seymour commented.

Klupkick turned to his pal Seymour, who was only his pal because he also started drinking at twelve noon on any given day of the week when he could, and was easily pushed around. And no one else would hang out with him.

"You'd screw anything," Klupkick spit out in a disgusted tone.

Seymour retorted in a defensive manner. "What? What's wrong with that? I hear them retard girls are real horny in the sack.

They don't have any a them hang ups like normal babes do."

Even Klupkick had to wince a little. "You're one sick fuck, you know that don't you? How do you figure that you can even call either of those two 'tarded split-tails a babe anyway? They probably don't clean themselves and I'd be afraid they're biters … they all are you know," Klupkick griped earnestly. He in his best tutorial tone. "You only get one mistake like that you know. I'd hate to have to call you Bobbit for the rest of your life."

The bartender just shook his head in disgust and went to the other end of the bar.

"Well if I get a chance to try I'll bet that one they call Sally is eager," Seymour finished.

By this time the Ferris House gang had moseyed over to their assigned lane and they were starting the process of settling in for an afternoon of bowling. Chico went confidently over to Antwan. He knew Antwan was his friend and was not afraid to ask for anything from him.

"When can we have our cheeseburgers Antwan?" Chico inquired.

Antwan smiled down to Chico. "Just wait until we get going with the first game, then we can go up to the snack bar and order for everyone. Ok pal? Why don't you help Clark find a ball, is that ok for you?" Antwan suggested in an amiable fashion.

"Sure," Chico grinned cheerfully.

"Good man," Antwan automatically replied.

Antwan busied himself with setting up the score sheet.

"Abigail would you like to handle the score sheet today?" he asked.

"I want ta bowl," Abigail cryptically stated.

"Are you sure hon? You don't sound so sure," Antwan urged.

Antwan patiently waited as Abigail thought this through. This process took about a dozen seconds. Clark fidgeted nervously while Sally was slowly tying her shoes. Abigail finally spoke up.

"No, I don't like to do the paper," Abigail emphasized. She exhibited her desire by shaking her head and waiving her hands in a warding off motion.

"Ok Abigail, no problem," Antwan conceded. "Sally, how about you?"

"I like to keep score Antwan," she answered happily.

"Well come on over it's your job today,"

Antwan motioned her to a chair.

Sally went over to the plastic chair and started to set up the score sheet.

"You guys finish getting situated while Chico and me go order lunch. Clark, please stay here with Sally and Abigail," Antwan said pointedly.

Clark stopped his compulsive, paranoid looking around at all the bowling alley's other patrons long enough to nod over to Antwan. Antwan had learned that Clark would eventually settle down to relax and enjoy his surroundings given a little time.

Antwan proceeded up to the snack bar with Chico walking beside him. A sociable lady behind the counter saw them coming.

"Hi guys, how is everyone doing today?" she asked.

"Good Hotch, how are the cheeseburgers today?" Antwan said.

"With fried onions," Chico put in quickly. He happily rubbed his hands together as he sometimes did, as though he were

Hotch laughed; she had a hearty laugh befitting her size. She was not a fat person but certainly a sturdy one with a stern but kind way about herself. She was of the variety of old school woman that had actually been a welder in an aircraft factory during World War II.

Because of her sturdy stock she was able to lie about her age and acquired work at the age of 15 while the men were off fighting the Nazis. She learned how to rivet and weld. Now she flips burgers at the bowling alley for a few extra bucks and to keep busy. She was a no nonsense sort of person that called them as she saw them and she saw them with both eyes dead on. No sugar coating for Hotch. Bar none she was also just as compassionate as she was tough. She was especially fond of Chico in that even with the dirty hand that she felt he had been dealt in life, he tried as hard and even harder than a lot of people she had encountered in her 68 plus years.

"So Chico you working hard these days?" Hotch asked in a warm conversational tone.

Chico looked over the counter at the food display of cakes, muffins, and various other goodies.

"I'm ok Hotch I g-g- got a new job at work."

"What's that?" Hotch asked.

She threw some burgers on the grill and began to prepare the rest of the platters for their lunch order.

Chico was distracted by a little girl walking past with her mother. She had a stuffed bear and stared at Chico with the curious innocence of youth. Chico smiled at her and waived his stubby fingers as he had seen other people do to little children. The mother pulled the child quickly away. Chico did not even realize that someone else might take offense at the very act the mother just performed, much less his act of kindness toward the child.

As the meat sizzled on the grill, Antwan glanced down the bowling alley to check on the rest of the group and saw they were all right. They were still struggling to get their shoes on. Antwan picked up a newspaper and started to scan the front page.

"Chico, you awake today?" Hotch asked.

Chico was drawn back to Hotch by her question and smiled again. "Huh? Oh, sorry Hotch, what?"

"You were telling me about your new job, remember?"

"Oh yeah I forgot." He looked back to the food on the other side of the counter. "I hand out different things at the store for people to try," he answered.

"Oh that's nice," Hotch said. In her effortless small talk tone she continued. "What are your hours?"

Chico stuttered a little bit. "Ell-ell-eleven in the morning to five at night, I-I-I work four days a week," Chico got out.

"Those aren't bad hours at all. When are your days off?" Hotch continued.

"Saturday, Sunday, a-and Monday," Chico was paying attention this time.

"Well that sounds like its good for you, you make some money too," Hotch answered plainly. She flipped the burgers and the fried onions over and began to put rolls on the grill.

"Yeah," Chico exclaimed. In a distracted but inflective manner he watched Hotch cook; mesmerized by the food on the grill and the delicious odors his nose was enmeshed in.

Hotch came over to the counter and leaned on it with both elbows. She fixed Antwan with a very frank gaze of her pale blue eyes.

"So you want coffee with your lunch Antwan?"

Antwan turned the page on the newspaper he was reading.

"Yeah Hotch that would be good, cream no sugar please."

"I'll have soda with my lunch Hotch," Chico interrupted.

"I kind'a figured that Chico," Hotch said mildly. "The same for the other ones Antwan or what?"

"Yeah, soda for all of them," he said matter-of-factly. "Anything that tastes sweet you know," He mumbled not even looking up from his newspaper.

As this exchange continued —down the way, at the bar, Seymour left his drinking buddy to 'shake the dew off his lily' as he referred to it. Seymour sauntered slowly past the group from Ferris House eyeballing Sally with his best macho look trying to catch her gaze. This of course failed as Sally was engrossed in doing an appropriate job on her assigned task. In the men's room as Seymour stood at the urinal doing 'the deed' as he thought of it, with all the wit he could muster, he moved arduously on to the next thought within his limited cognitive progression. *"That one retard girl looks pretty good,"* he thought to himself as he daydreamed about her.

He had seen her around and she seemed to be a good sport. He could tell because she, Sally, he thought was her name, was always smiling and had an easy laugh. And she looked almost normal. Not that this was an over burdensome prerequisite for Seymour as Seymour never had good luck with many women in the past...

He was about twenty-four years old and still remembered with tremendous male-ego busting embarrassment and humiliation his last attempt with the fairer sex.

Seymour was not a very attractive looking man, certainly not the jock-Hollywood good looks of many of the athletes at his high school. Seymour also was not an athlete, nor come to think of it did he have exemplary hygiene to boot. He could have brushed his teeth a little more often and it wouldn't have hurt to wash his greasy hair more than once a week—and maybe a hair cut.

Many of the girls at high school looked upon him with disdain and much of the time open revulsion. This certainly did not go unnoticed by Seymour and he was not unaffected by their ridicule, being at that degree of sensitivity as most were in that period of their development.

It was his senior year and Seymour was not antisocial, but he was better around men as opposed to women. And he was a follower not a leader. He would hunt during hunting season and play some sports but did not excel in any of them.

He came from a single parent family; his father left his mother many years before and Seymour could barely remember him. If anyone got to know his mother very well they obviously understand why the father had left. But that did not give good reason as to why he did not pay child support.

Clare Hinkel, Seymour's mother, had been abused as a child and therefore had passed it on to her family. She had been demeaned to the point of profound neurosis and could never do anything right, or so she was told.

Like any child she craved her parents attention no matter how negative. Any attention was better than none. She would do things to make those around her angry. Even to this day if she did not get enough attention she would just piss someone off to get her share. This created a very dysfunctional atmosphere that was a breeding ground for negative feelings which eventually turned to abuse. Clare would use the same warped, demeaning technique on her son with effective results.

Needless to say, by the time Seymour got around to senior prom time he was totally screwed up as far as his inter-personal skills went. Then miraculously along came Rita Johnson, the almost love of his life.

She was a sheltered girl, not too intelligent, a little slow some might say, but nice. Rita had mousy brown hair, brown eyes, and a petite frame; lean almost to the point of anorexia. She had a very gentle personality and was terribly shy. No one bothered with Rita much; she was clumsy around people, as many were at that age.

From the first day Seymour laid eyes on Rita he was totally smitten. Seymour was only a notch or two above Rita in the high school social hierarchy, which was as low on the food chain one could get without being constantly harassed by the bullies that frequented school systems.

So when it came time to go to the prom Seymour felt the stirrings of enough teenage hormonal courage to ask Rita out. He promised himself that regardless of whatever type of abuse his mother was going to portion out when she found out about this transgression, he had to break out from under her utter control. That the ill treatment he received would be well worth the attention of Rita Johnson. Or so he assured himself.

Seymour carefully chose the day, practiced his lines and put on his coolest set of clothing. He left home before his mother was able to question him and notice that he was preoccupied with something other than her.

Rita was not so slow that she did not notice Seymour's hankering stare or how he would try to strike up conversations with her. So when Seymour made his move and sat down at her secluded lunch table she was accepting of, as well as apprehensive with, his company.

Seymour, also being nervous, did not do well. He forgot all the well practiced lines and began to stutter. Just when his head was about to explode with frustration Rita moved in and accepted his offer of a prom date.

The night of the prom Seymour was finally able to get out of his house. And much to his mother's chagrin and spiteful attempts to shame him into submission, he valiantly made his way on his newly designated path to his shining destiny.

Alas, from the first, the long-awaited night was a disaster. But the very worst came when he tried to make a pass at Rita. He was a clumsy buffoon, and when they were finally alone Seymour misunderstood all the signals and it ended up as just another date rape incident. Needless to say a hell-storm followed and Seymour was imbued with a reputation as a sexual predator. This followed him around the local area until this day, not to mention the damage that was done to Rita.

Subsequently, instead of returning to the bar, Seymour had built up an early lead on his alcohol buzz. Consequently, with all this baggage trailing him like a black cloud (which incidentally helped to develop his reputation as a pervert) this also made what was about to transpire a kind of self-fulfilling prophecy.

Seymour set out from the bathroom and made a bee line over to the lanes where Sally was patiently waiting for lunch to arrive before they started their game. Utilizing his courage in a can, Seymour walked up to the rail behind the seats, leaned on it, and gave a disgusting leer toward Sally.

Seymour considered this his best come-hither look; he knew no babe could resist. Clark, who finally had sat down on the plastic benches so common to bowling alleys was facing the pins and was the first to feel this peril resembling a sinister storm cloud developing behind them. Sally was painstakingly filling out the score sheet.

Seymour burped, slowly rubbed his paunch and spoke up. "Hey there beautiful, brains and beauty too huh?" Seymour slyly used a line he had heard in a movie.

Abigail and Sally looked over at Seymour, with an expression of guilty confusion, one that had been ingrained into them from years of being in the system. They felt as though they were caught doing something sinfully wrong, but didn't know what.

"Your name's Sally, ain't it? I seen you around. Want to go for a ride? I got a truck out front, we could have some fun. You got the need to breed?" Seymour posed in depraved fashion. "I do," he finished, wit oozing from him.

Abigail started to mutter to herself in a sing-song fashion. Sally giggled nervously, not knowing how to react. Her good nature had kept her innocent in many ways, her grasp almost akin to a kindergartner.

Seymour came around the rail—down into the pit. Clark jumped up frantically, anxiously trying to look in all directions at once. Seymour proceeded over, ignoring Clark and Abigail, and stood directly beside Sally. Towering over her with his greasy presences, he made his move.

"Come on honey, let's go," Seymour crudely slurred out.

He took the pencil out of her hand and put it on the table.

Sally looked up with alarm in her eyes from where she sat in the chair. She finally found the courage to speak up.

"I can't go nowhere with you, Mister. We're bowling today," Sally sheepishly, confusedly told Seymour as her only means of defense.

Seymour grabbed her right arm below the shoulder with his left hand, and tried gently at first to guide her out of the chair. Abigail's mumbling became louder and she started to punch her knee, hard. Sally became almost hysterical— while at the same time Clark snapped. He did not think, he acted.

He leapt toward Seymour, but then stopped short, almost realizing that he was never aggressive—he was a natural coward, afraid of his own shadow. He began to do the only thing he could do.

"SSSSStop ThThThThat LLLLet GGo of SSSally," he sputtered.

People in adjacent lanes had been politely ignoring the group, but now turned and stared in shock and disgust. Now Seymour began to get nervous and a little pissed off at this other retard trying to move in on his chosen babe. He was too intoxicated and stupid in his single-mindedness to just walk away.

"What the hell's going on over there?" a person from the next pit spoke up.

Seymour, now acting completely irrationally, (not that he ever was very rational to start with), pulled Sally out of the chair.

"Come on, you retard girl, we're going for a ride," he mumbled pointedly.

Sally started to cry.

People in nearby pits started to grumble.

"Damn white trash, can't even go bowling on a Saturday. Why don't they keep them people out of public places?" intoned a patron.

"Let her go, pervert," another remark.

Meager clarity started to turn to all out pandemonium in Seymour's partially pickled brain.

All of a sudden a heavy hand fell on his shoulder and Seymour was jerked away from Sally so violently that he actually for an instant came off his feet. He was turned around too quickly to even get dizzy, and looked up into the glowering face of Antwan.

"What are doing son?" Antwan grumbled in a dangerously low voice.

The instant Antwan's questions escaped his lips, Fred McBride, the owner of the bowling alley, whom no one realized had arrived in the pit, piped up.

"The police will be here in five minutes, gentleman. You, big boy, let go of him and try to calm your people down, you're ruining my business. Seymour!" Fred fired in a voice smooth like steel.

"Sit down right over here in this chair—now! I'm sure Officer Scott is going to want to talk to you," he finished.

Seymour complied meekly, afraid of Fred. Fred turned to Antwan and talked patiently never taking his eyes from him.

"Marcia tells me your name is Antwan."

Antwan was trying to calm Sally down as Chico, who had left the lunches forgotten on the back table, was trying to talk to Clark, who was by now stuttering nonsensical gibberish, unable to articulate.

Clark's face was going through strange contortions which made it look as though he were possessed.

Chico was scared; he had never seen Clark like this.

"Its o-o-o-k-k-k Cl-Cl-Clark, Antwan is here," Chico stuttered out fearfully.

Clark himself knew on some level beneath his panic attack that he hadn't been like this in decades. Not since he was preyed upon at the institution by some of the other inmates. At that time he had little or no protection afforded to him from the staff.

The hideous panic from the old days that used to swamp his timid personality started to take hold of his shattered psyche. He felt as though he would lose control and have his head explode —his mind started to shut down—retreat to that dark place of inexorable insanity from which there was no escape, no return. He had been in that nightmarish place too many times in his life. He knew with inevitable surety that he would not escape the old horror! Not this time, he was much older and a lot less resilient than he had been 20 years ago. His vision actually began to go dark at the outer edges of his sight, as if he were drowning.

All of a sudden Antwan put a reassuringly calm hand on his shoulder.

"Take a breath Clark."

Clark did. He mentally grabbed onto the proffered lifeline.

"Good, take another breath, Clark," Antwan encouraged reassuringly, calmly.

Clark took another. This helped to regulate his panic attack. Clark had come to trust Antwan in the short time he had known him.

"Sit over here and keep breathing; I'll fix everything," Antwan said in his calm baritone voice.

Antwan had never betrayed Clark; his eyes blinked like a strobe light, he nodded his understanding and sat in the designated chair.

"Marcia tells me that your name is Antwan," Fred repeated.

Antwan looked over to Fred, and he went back to shushing Sally as he sat her down in a chair.

"That's right," Antwan rumbled over his shoulder to Fred. "You must be Mr. McBride. We've never met before but my name is Antwan Strong."

The situation was beginning to defuse. Fred looked around at the other patrons who had gathered around the disturbance.

"Everyone please get back to their lanes," he recommended.

One of the bowling alley patrons that had participated in the town meeting last year (attempting to exercise his civic duty), also known as a chronic complainer, piped up, adding salt to the wound.

"You know Fred it's hard to enjoy ourselves with people like this around."

"You can't possibly mean these people, you must mean the perv' alcoholic," someone else contended argumentatively back to the complainer.

They started to get into a squabble.

"If you two don't want to talk to Officer Scott also, you should go back to your lanes," McBride suggested to them.

"Maybe I'll just stop coming here," one said as they walked away.

"What ever mills your wheat," Fred thought to himself as he turned his back on them.

He again turned to confront Antwan who was standing patiently, directing Chico to pass out the lunches.

"Mister Strong," he patiently explained to Antwan. "I'm as tolerant as the next guy is, but you have to keep your people under control or you can't come here anymore."

"This young lady," Antwan calmly stated. "Was just assaulted in your establishment we have no other choice but to press charges against your friend over there from the bar."

McBride rolled his eyes. “What a stinkin' mess. Mister Strong, next time do me a favor and take your people to a movie…”

That night, things were as normal as was possible at Ferris House. Chico was busily working on the computer; Hector was in his usual spot in the corner gently rocking back and forth.

Darla poked her head in the room. “How are you doing Chico? Do you need any help with that?”

“No Darla, I just take my time like Dave showed me,” Chico smiled in return.

“OK don’t be too late, if you need anything I’ll be going over the goals books in the dining room then I’m going home.”

Darla looked at Hector for a moment. “Don’t stay up too late Hector,” she disappeared from the doorway.

Hector seemed content as he watched Chico on the computer and gave no apparent reply that he heard her, although by coincidence he tapped his chest twice as he rocked.

Chico slowly and methodically two-finger-typed a message to his friend Chucky on the computer. “Hi Chucky how are you?” *Enter.*

A few minutes later the message came back.

“We had a gud time today we wnt to the movie and saw the Cat in the Hat.”

Chico slowly typed his return message. This took a few minutes as he was trying to be careful like Dave showed him.

“We went bowling but got into trouble.” *Enter.*

After few minutes the reply materialized in from Chucky.

“Didn’t they like you at the bowling ally?”

Chico slowly read the message out loud and moved his lips as he did. He looked up at the ceiling as he thought, then slowly started to type again.

“Marisa is nice she gives us our shoes and Hotch maks us our lunch, I like her alot shes my friend. A guy from the barr tried to hurt Sally.” *Enter.*

Chico also mumbled “enter” every time he hit the key. A little longer time went by before Chico got a reply. This time Chico thought that maybe Chucky fell asleep as he had done so before. Suddenly the message came through.

: (“did you cal the polise?” Chucky’s message asked.

Hector was closer to the computer and rocked faster. Chico did not notice him as he was getting into telling the story.

"no," he typed, "Antwan got mad at the guy and stoped him but the manager calld the cops." :) *Enter.*

The story wound on for another hour or so before Chico got tired and signed off, but he again left the computer running. Hector was right behind him as he started to get up out of the chair. Chico was startled by Hector's proximity.

"Hector!! Don't sneak up on me like that, you scared me. Come on, let's go to bed," Chico said.

Chico took Hector's hand to guide him but Hector again did not want to go and pulled away swiftly. He began to rock even more violently.

"Fine stay here, I'm going to bed," Chico mumbled in slight consternation.

Chico left Hector in the computer room and knew as with many times prior he would go to bed when he was ready.

Hector was staring at the computer monitor, mesmerized. He rocked gently back and forth as if he could stay there the rest of the night. As he relaxed into his gentle rocking mode (almost as if he were practicing a meditative art), his mind drifted back once again to his long past childhood at the institution.

After being torn from his home Hector continued to have a tumultuous existence at the state institution. For the first 10 years, Hector had all he could do to survive in the wards at Willowbrook. His consciousness became nothing more than a shrewd wild animal trying to survive in a jungle society. The trauma of his displacement from the only secure place he had known for the first five years of his life, and his mother's remembered love, never left him.

He was aware that attendants tried to care for him. But bathing him with hoses and throwing him his clothes did not seem to encourage a very nurturing upbringing. They would then herd him off to the cafeteria to compete for food with the other inmates. But this was like feeding time on the Serengeti Plain; always a fight to eat his food before his peers got a hold of his meager share.

The larger, stronger ones of the group would sometimes steal his food and he would pay the price if he tried to stop them.

The staff who tried to help, actually endeavoring to do their job as opposed to those simply there for a paycheck, numbered too few and were always exhausted. This was why he ate so fast when he sat down to a meal even to this day.

The attacks from the stronger and more aggressive inmates, both sexual and the more straightforward beatings, also took their toll on him. The attendants, as a rule, of course tried to break these up, but again were so understaffed that this was not always possible in an expedient fashion. And they could not be there all of the time.

His perception of the world around him was profoundly different than those of the regulars who had taken care of him at Willowbrook. Many of his simple experiences were pure torture. Even though he interacted with these people on a daily basis, the few good individuals that wanted to help were completely out of their league. 'Regular' was how he thought of them as his comprehension advanced. They had no idea of his unlocked potential or even that it existed. How could they? He was so sensitive he could almost feel emotion, and sometime actually did as a physical sensation. His physiological senses were processed differently than a normal person. Rough clothing did not only cause itching but outright pain; as if he were wearing coarse sand-paper. Certain sounds and frequencies were intolerable. Where normal people may only find them an annoyance or simply tune them out. Consequently, many of Hector's perceptions were not the accepted model and certainly not even thought of by the experts until years later.

His existence continued like this for ten years, living in filth, sometimes fighting with the other inmates in animalistic fashion simply for some food or safety. The simple amenities of existence were rare for him. He got only occasional attention and periodic medical treatment. Hector also learned to protect himself with bluster and fakery, like a blowfish. Some of these horrible abuses and sexual brutalities got past his bluffs, and of course affected him deeply.

He didn't realize it at the time, but in 1972 a tremendous turning point in his life materialized with the expose done on Willowbrook by Geraldo. By then he was 15 years old. The only thing he really noticed was that there were more people around and they seemed kinder. It cost him less pain with their endeavors toward him.

He eventually was transferred to Letchworth adult ward at the age of 21 and came in contact with many other people. He learned Spanish from some of the Puerto Rican patients who lived in Letchworth Village. He learned Yiddish from some of his retarded Hebrew compatriots who resided with him. Hector understood three languages, eerily, by the age of 24 although he was never able to speak a word.

Hector was a brilliant person and no one ever knew it. He began to learn more than just the survival skills he had learned on the children's ward. Recreation specialists would come to the wards and try to engage the residents in various activities. He could feel their compassion; it wasn't a painful sensation as the earlier, coarser people's attitudes had been. They taught him games, they showed him pictures of the outside world, and they stimulated his brain. And although he couldn't communicate the things he learned from them through these activities, his brain soaked up everything like a parched desert plain during a torrential tropical rain.

He began to learn exponentially about a far greater existence outside of his inward looking world. More than he had ever endeavored to imagine. Hector began to realize that he had been locked in a prison almost all his life. These were some of the life experiences and incidental tortures which were brought to Ferris House by Hector.

As Hector stood there in front of the computer watching the screen saver, the lines of changing color and pattern gave him great pleasure. Hector was able to project the random patterns in his mind's eye before they happened because after all they were not arbitrary, they ran off a program. Once he studied the patterns, he could guess the program's direction. And no one, not even Hector (at the time); suspected the innate cleverness that was his gift…

7
Free at Last
(Finally something good happens)

Monday arrived with surprisingly little fanfare. Everyone from Ferris House could relax and go back to work from a weekend that was more eventful than they imagined it could be.

Elsewhere in a nearby town, there was another day program in the process of gearing up for the day's routine. Abigail and Sally attended this one as opposed to the one that Hector, Clark, and Ike attended. This allegedly was due to the perceived fact that they all had different levels of function.

A constant flow of vans pulled up to the main entrance of the building and disgorged their human cargo, then drove away. Bleary eyed, mostly medicinally-zombieized people sluggishly wandered through the front door to their daily labors. Like gray clad automatons in some totalitarian sci-fi futuristic movie, they obediently filed in and took their assigned positions.

Nancy Boorsman pulled into a parking space at the other side of the parking lot from where the vans were unloading.

"Ok girls we're here, everybody out!"

Abigail and Sally struggled to get their lunch coolers and open the car door. Nancy patiently waited. After ten seconds or so the women got out and headed toward the main entrance.

"Have a good day, we'll see you after work," Nancy called after them.

"What are we having for dinner tonight, Nancy?" Sally asked.

"Tuna casserole," Nancy answered, "is that good?"

"I like tuna casserole," Sally said. She softly smiled and rushed after Abigail.

Inside they proceeded past the receptionist window where a very hefty woman was seated. The woman took another bite of her coffee cake.

"Good morning girls," the woman said in a blasé manner. "Better hurry, Charlene is getting everything set up in your work area."

Abigail and Sally rush past, automatically saying "Good morning," acting as though they felt guilty for doing something wrong but didn't know what.

In the work area, there were two dozen adults with varied disabilities attempting to get situated so they could begin their day's labor. Most of them frantically stumble around as though their very lives depended on their performance for their overlords, or suffer the consequences.

Charlene, one of the program assistants, firmly addressed the room as though she were addressing a new batch of trainees at boot camp.

"Come on everyone, let's go, we should be working already! Sally I don't want to see any stuff like you did last week."

Sally blushed and quietly took her seat trying to become an unobtrusive part of the surroundings.

"Jeremy you neither," Charlene said sternly.

Jeremy gave Charlene 'the finger' when she turned her back on him. A few of the other people in the work shop who saw what Jeremy did chuckled quietly.

"Settle down," Charlene automatically barked out.

She headed for her desk, her back still to the room. The assemblage began to settle down and everyone got to work.

Abigail appeared to be having difficulty getting into her task. She was distracted and did not really like to do what had been deemed her assigned drudgery. She stared off into space, not for the first time, and experienced flashes of her earliest memories. Although she was now 39 years old, bits and pieces of her life prior to Ferris House comprised despair and a gray hopeless feeling of detachment.

She remembered being carried in the arms of a young woman, one whose face she did not and could not remember, one with no expectation of goodness in life, one in a constant state of dejection. The scrawny miserable individual who was her mother had her despair compounded by the heavy falling snow as she slogged through dirty un-shoveled sidewalks on a cold, gray, winter morning.

Abigail was virtually born at the steps of a brick building in a run down section in Rochester, N. Y. After some few years on the street with her mother, they were taken in and given warmth and transient security by the nuns at a Catholic orphanage. Her mother was not well, physically or emotionally; these feelings were transferred directly over to Abigail.

In 1963, not very much was known about the ravages of substance abuse. Consequently proper care was not given to pregnant drug addicts. Therefore her mother committed suicide before the following spring arrived. This left Abigail four years old and functionally abandoned.

Due to the lack of parental stimulation necessary to the early psycho-social development of any child, coupled with the effects of fetal alcohol syndrome disorder, Abigail had a pitiful start in life. Consequently, as time passed, she was deemed retarded by the well meaning but firm nuns and lay people of the Rochester orphanage. And since they had little experience at the time with the devastation and effects of her issues, little effort was given to her further educational development. These were not bad people, they just didn't know.

Although she was a bright young child, she was tentative of her unknown abilities and therefore did not have the benefit of the doubt given people with disabilities decades later. fortunately there were remarkably compassionate people who attempted to work with her and educate her along the way. Couple this with the more stern people that tried to control and force her into a mold which she was incapable of fitting, and here she was.

This type of carrot and stick development continued for about three more years until she was six years old. At this point she was given over to the state system and parked in a Letchworth children's ward. There, at the age of thirteen, she was raped by a nightshift employee (who had a preference for young children). This, along with various other abuses, went on for some time until she became pregnant and had to have an abortion.

All this occurred around 1972 and about that time more light was being shed on the abuses and neglect which disabled people were experiencing in the system.

Eventually with the restructuring within the system she, along with some others, were transferred to private agencies or state-run community residences.

This cost the state a lot less tax payer dollars. Abigail's luck of the draw, her happy destiny, would land her eventually with her new extended family at Ferris House. This would be the first family ambience she had ever experienced in her life…

These were some of the thoughts which were struggling through her mind at the precise time of her first mistake. Abigail was having a bad day to start with. The doctor decided to try her on a new blood pressure medication, which had doped her up pretty badly. This in turn played havoc with her already poor motor skills. To top it all off Sandy, the employee working in her section, had been out partying much too late the night before and could have been a little more patient. So when she upset the tray of product that she was working on, Sandy with the hangover rolled her eyes.

"You did that on purpose Abigail; clean that up before I write you up," Sandy demanded.

Abigail, properly humiliated, tried to push back from the table and upset another tray of product. By this time she was in a panic. Abigail tried to turn around and tripped over her chair. She fell to the floor hitting her head on the hard tile with a very satisfying thump, like a honeydew melon on cement— happy Monday.

"Shit," was the first word that escaped Sandy's mouth. "Abigail you are a real pain in the ass, now we have to go to the nurse," Sandy commented contemptuously.

"AAAAiiieeerrr my head," Abigail screamed. "It hurts, I'm sorry, it hurts."

"Shut up damn-it-all, **Charlene I need you over here now!"** Sandy hollered.

Charlene made her way over to Abigail's table.

"Sandy, go get the first-aid kit," Charlene snapped angrily. She was pissed-off at the amount of paperwork that would now be coming her way.

"Here Abigail, sit up, stop crying or we can't help you," she said impatiently.

Abigail worked down to quiet sobs as she held her head even more humiliated if that was possible. She started to hum one of her mindless tunes and began to rock painfully back and forth.

Sandy came back with the first aid kit and handed it over to Charlene. Charlene broke open a cold pack and applied it to Abigail's head. This eventually calmed her down further.

"Sandy," Charlene said. "Take her to the nurse; I'll call her house to get someone to come pick her up. Also write it up as a behavior so we can maybe get something to keep her calmer when the report hits the higher-ups."

Charlene proceeded in the direction of the office.

Sandy's voice followed her. "She was looking for trouble from the word go, she had a shitty attitude," Sandy stated defensively.

"Just do it, Sandy, I've got more important things to worry about," Charlene retorted. Miserably, Abigail accompanied Sandy to the nurse, humiliation plain on her face.

"This week is not off to a good start," Sandy grumbled as she assisted Abigail…

Nurse Quinn was sitting at her desk playing tic-tac-toe on her desk blotter. She glanced up as the two came in to her office.

"Teresa," Sandy whined. "I'm sorry I got some work for you."

"Oh, here they come again," Teresa remarked. She was trying to make her statement sound humorous hoping it would put Abigail at ease. "Abigail I just saw you here a few weeks ago. What did you do this time?"

Abigail stood looking down at her feet ashamed and humiliated, arms askew as though she were a captured prisoner.

"Yeah, she had a little behavior; we'll have to write this one up too," Sandy injected.

For a brief moment they both stared disapprovingly at Abigail, she flashed back to the Catholic orphanage in Rochester. Good old Catholic-guilt incessantly rose up in her along with the double whammy of the persecution permitted on those with disabilities.

Abigail was in a dark mood. She continued to hum a tune as she allowed them to put her through the processes that an injured retard must undergo. Especially from insensitive staff; listening to them talk about her as though she weren't there. Simply another piece of furniture that had to be dusted off and put in its proper place in the room.

Certainly not a person with feelings and desires which were in anyway similar to theirs.

She knew the routine well. Someone from the house would come and pick her up and take her to the emergency room; she'll be subjected to further humiliations. Then she would finally be taken home to Ferris House where she knew she would eventually achieve the solace and safety of her own room. There at least she could simmer on this embarrassment and start to forget. Simply another humiliation that plagued her in a long line of humiliations she had suffered throughout a crappy lifetime.

Across town at Hector's program, although he wasn't having an exemplary day, it was not too bad. Fred was no longer employed there. He heard Connie talking to Elmer on the phone earlier and garnered from the conservation that a 'paper trail' had finally caught up with Fred. It seemed that everyone was more relaxed, staff and client alike. This gave Hector breathing room to try to do his work with less pressure. As he worked, his thoughts wandered back once again his previous existence.

Although Hector didn't recognize his inability to breach his internal mind's wall as frustration, he did certainly feel the emotion intensely. With his new taste of the world around him, he endeavored to understand everything. He learned English perfectly from those around him, on a university level. This was all he had to do with his time, to learn from those around him. As care improved for him over the years he came more and more in contact with eminently educated and more qualified people as they evaluated, studied, and attempted to learn more about autism and its consequences.

As they learned about him, he learned about them. They never realized that his IQ, if they were able to measure it, was of the genius level. He learned many things from watching television and listening to the radio. He learned all about the world around him in the late 70s and the 80s, all of course through the prism of the American media.

Throughout all these years of trials, tribulations, and much much personal pain, coupled with some little pleasure, Hector had communicate what he had learned had to have an outlet. This lack of a vent became more apparent and began to exhibit itself through accelerated physical behaviors. After all, Hector was only human.

His perceptions of the world around him were skewed by his affliction with autism. For instance, he didn't always see everyone at eye-level like normal people did. His brain through its disability sometimes compelled him to perceive some of life's events as though he were looking down on them from several feet above. This was one of several alternate perceptions that he had to deal with resulting from his yoke of autism. Another quirk was the perception of pain and pleasure he felt through the expression of people's emotions of love or hate, compassion or brutality. These emotions he felt in his heart as many of us do, but he also felt them as physical sensations, like a slap in the face, or the warmth and pleasurable reassurance of a friend's hand on one's shoulder. In spite of all this adversity, Hector's indomitable spirit carried him through.

Sure he had his bloody battle scars, and they manifested themselves through the pitiful keening and the self-destructive physical abuses he wrought on his person. The doctors tried to give him medication to soothe his emotional pain and curb his violent tendencies. Although these medications sedated him, they did nothing to allay his frustrations or his inability to communicate with the outside world.

By the mid 80s the powers-that-be in academia had convinced the political machine that it would be better (and cheaper) for people like Hector not to live in institutions, but to live in houses in the community. Someone had the bright idea that if you treat all these people in institutions as though they were more normal, that they may actually act more normal. This process was a matter of degree. Start with the easy stuff first, get them out of the institutions; get them into a way of life more similar to the one with which we're familiar. But it became even more than that. Before you got them out of the institutions and into houses in the greater community you also had to treat them as though they were actually people. Person centered planning was created.

For Hector this was a far cry from what they told his parents back in 1962: put him away and forget about him. But by end of 1997 Hector was out of an institutional type setting and in a house on a rural road in a neighborhood just like any other, along with five other people, three men, two women. Each suffering from various gradations and combinations of mental or physical disability. This place was manifestly known by most as Ferris House …

Chico was off work today, at home. He was happy. No job coach was around asking him stupid questions or telling him how to do the job he already knew how to do, or worse yet, embarrassing him in front of his customers.

Chico knew the job coach meant well, but he didn't feel as though he even needed her around anymore. There were always regulars around. One thing Chico longed for, and it took some time for him to realize this, was that he would rather be left alone at his job just like every other person in the world who worked. Just let him work.

Chico was watching TV in his room. Elmer was down in the office working, Nunzia,who worked days today, had gone to pick up Abigail at program. Chico heard them say that Abigail had injured herself. He hoped that she would be all right. He liked everyone in his extended family at Ferris House. Not that they sometimes didn't argue, that, he remembered, was how it was sometimes when he lived with his real family a long time ago.

Chico had been the youngest of six. Being disabled put more pressure on the family than they were easily able to handle. Eventually his father skipped out, leaving only his mother with six children, one of them seemingly seriously disabled. For a single mother, the burden eventually became too much.

Although Chico's eldest sister Maria helped him a lot, the family could not keep up. Chico's mother finally admitted Chico to Letchworth Villages Children's Unit in 1960 against the wishes of Maria. This drove a wedge into the family from which it would never completely recover.

Chico was devastated. He had undeniably come to love his mother and his siblings just like any five year would. Because of this trauma he was very fortunate to have survived the next 15 years as well as he did. But by the time his 20th birthday rolled around he had adjusted quite well.

Chico was only 4' 5," typical for someone with his type of Affliction. But posture was not the only physiological concern for a Downs Syndrome person. Other problems would shorten his life. But with the advent of modern medicine much of this could be combated. He and others like him could and did live much longer, more comfortable lives. Fortunately, Chico had a good-natured personality and was well liked by many of the attendants on the wards he had inhabited over the years. He liked to help out doing menial labor. Chico worked in the laundry and also helped with the cleaning which any institutional setting required.

He never forgot his mother and family, though. She did eventually begin to visit him ten years after his admission. By then, of course, his other siblings were self-sufficient and scattered far around the country as sometimes happened in today's modern world. It also helped that the social worker had contacted his mother after Chico's repeated requests over the years.

The first reunion had been very difficult. But it had developed over the next several years into a relationship where his mother was actually able to bring him home on holidays and other special occasions. This of course was a great joy to Chico. This went on for another decade until his mother died of cancer. Maria, his sister, also had met with tragedy in a car accident a few years after his original admission into Letchworth. She had tried to visit him but her mother would not take her and as a minor she was not permitted onto the wards. Chico found this out early on in his mother's visits. This event had added pain to Chico's already flagellated being, which he found difficult to handle. But his indomitable spirit endured. To boot, none of the other siblings had attempted any contact with Chico—ever.

At his mother's funeral he did come in contact with his father, who after deserting his family had made a reasonably successful business for himself in Florida doing landscaping maintenance. Chico's likeable personality and yearning for love eventually won his father over. Maybe the years of guilt helped also.

By the time Chico was 43 years old he came to live at Ferris House with Hector. Coincidentally, not long after that his father started to have him to his house on vacation several times a year. Maybe the social worker that contacted his father to get permission to move him to a community residence also had something to do with this.

But it did not matter to Chico how his father came back into his life, only that he had. He held down a part-time job cleaning up at a local factory and was quite happy with this because much of the time he was able to consider himself normal.

Eventually he wanted to change jobs and was assisted in doing so through Disabled People of America's Supported Employment Department. Now he handed out samples in a local grocery store and enjoyed interacting with the customers who frequented the store. These were some of the thoughts that Chico pondered as he also enjoyed his new found privacy at Ferris House…

8
Welcome Back (More Good News)

Sally was happy. Not just happy but exalted. Another difficult week had gone by with the usual degradations, abuses and humiliations. But Sally had weathered them with her typical good spirits and resiliency. Even so, on top of it all she had just learned that they were going to be able to keep Shadoe. Sally could not remember when she had been this excited about something. It was like Christmas, when she was very young, before she had been put out of her parents house and into institutionalized exile.

The excitement had spread through virtually everyone in the house like a potent virus. At least for the people who resided there. Contagious excitement among the residents had begun to strengthen inadvertently the bonds that made Ferris House a real home and for those that resided there, a family.

Anyone who had not shared in the excitement had gone unnoticed by Sally, and there were a few. The wheels had turned in the machine of the powers that be, the machine that made the decisions at Disabled People of America, Inc. As long as it was deemed that the dog, Shadoe, was a good fit by those that managed the house and safe for all involved, that said dog would be an asset to the normal socialization, and beneficial to the greater good for those who live at Ferris House.

So Shadoe could stay. Of course, not everyone was happy about this decision to bring Shadoe into the house. Samantha argued vehemently against the dog living there and Nunzia only looked upon Shadoe as more work for her to do. As for the residents, Clark who was generally quiet and shy, especially after the bowling alley incident, Chico who was more extroverted and resilient than some, and Abigail whose reactions sometimes did not seem to fit the events, All seemed to have a new sense of anticipation. Whenever Shadoe's name was mentioned, even Hector showed various degrees of excitement.

Through their personal needs and paths of expression they would all welcome Shadoe into the house as one of them.

This very moment Darla was out with the van on her way to pick up Shadoe from her temporary exile, in what Darla called doggie prison. Clark and Chico went with her to assist and keep an eye on Shadoe.

The rest of the house was trying to do their late Saturday morning chores with Samantha, but had little success. They could not stay on task due to the atmosphere of exuberance. Samantha was in a foul mood. Sally and Abigail sensed this easily, and Hector kept his distance. He was out around the back of the house in imagined safety. Hector had been keeping his distance anyhow after the skullduggery of the other day.

When Darla or someone else Hector trusted was in the room he stayed in the area contentedly. But if it was just Samantha, Hector kept his distance and no one else seemed to notice. For her part, Samantha did not push the issue. She was obviously just happy to have gotten away with her criminal treatment of Hector and Ike, for now.

As Samantha smoked a cigarette and over-lorded the ladies trying to concentrate on the clean up around the dumpster, she didn't display the anxiety she felt. Not that she was guilt in what she had done to Hector, or Ike, it was simply that she did not want to get caught. And of course as far as she was concerned they had very well deserved what they got from her.

On the other hand, she was easily able to fool Ike into thinking that they were friends now. This new behavior by Samantha had not gone unnoticed by Darla or some of the other staff. But the general consensus was that maybe Samantha was coming around and had developed a new insight that would assist her with this type of human service job. Ike, for his part, was able to put the incident with Samantha quickly into the past.

Now when Samantha wanted something from Ike, she would ask him very sweetly. Needless to say Ike, being a reasonable man was happy to comply, as anyone would be when asked politely. As he swept the back patio Ike was talking to himself, as he was sometimes apt to do. Happily he mumbled about Hector.

"Ohh, yoouuu Hector, how come youuu'rre not working," he said to himself quietly.

He methodically tried to do a good job on the back patio. Ike's coordination was poor, but he doggedly worked on sweeping the back patio, he wanted it clean for Shadoe. There was no rancor in his statements as could be told by his affect and tone. Many times when Ike was by himself and otherwise occupied, he simply verbalized about the things going on around him. Half of the time he didn't even realize he did this. The other half of the time he didn't fret about it. For him it was like singing a song to himself.

Hector for his part was up at his favorite spot rocking back and forth gently as he watched for the lady with the auburn hair. He waited for her to come out into her rose garden. They all diligently did their work as best they could and awaited the grand moment. Except for Samantha, who generally adored supervising others when she was not on the Internet searching for new recipes in order to arouse her passionate culinary appetites. An hour passed.

Hector was the first one to see the van coming down the road. He dashed down to the edge of the driveway. As the van was pulling in, Sally, Abigail, and even Ike, who had learned to react to Hector's reflexes, all dropped what they were doing. The recognition that transformed to excitement as the van pulled to a stop in the parking space overtook them all, all except Samantha. The windows were open and Shadoe was excitedly wagging her tail and barking. Clark and Chico had very little ability to control Shadoe due to her enthusiasm. Chico just opened the door and Shadoe bounded out, running up to the residents of Ferris House. Chico and Clark struggled out of their seat belts as quickly as they were able and joined the happy bunch. Darla finally got out of the van as a joyful pandemonium ensued. Samantha had a sneer on her face as she puffed her cigarette, but kept her distance.

Shadoe was running around trying to greet everyone at the same time, also couldn't contain her doggy rapture.

All of a sudden as they petted and greeted her, Shadoe happily broke loose and excitedly ran all around the front yard in a big circle, expending the two weeks of pent-up energy and expressing her joy at being with her friends in her new home once again.

She ran up to Samantha and stopped two feet away head down slowly wagging her tail. Samantha froze with trepidation. Everyone paused to see what would happen. Shadoe eased up and sniffed Samantha's foot then her lower leg and sneezed out a great doggy sneeze on Samantha's pant leg. She then ran back to a more accepting group of friends.

"Dog snot, just what I needed," Samantha exclaimed disgustedly. But she relaxed a little as Shadoe obviously accepted her by not snarling at her.

"Alright everyone, alright, calm down," Darla raised her voice in a kind fashion. "Let's get Shadoe settled in and work out what we're going to do the rest of the day."

"I'm hungry," Ike said in a slow melodious voice as he turned to Samantha.

"Me too," chimed in Chico.

The others joined in and started to profess their hunger as well.

"Let's clean up our tools we can finish this after lunch," Darla recommended.

Samantha was already on her way into the house, intent on her favorite pastime. Soon the others trailed behind her and found their way into the house, where Samantha was already looking at the lunch schedule on the wall.

"Ike and Chico, you guys help me prepare the lunch. We're having cold cuts, sandwiches, and milk and juice,"

Samantha ordered out in her most congenial manner.

"Hector it's your turn to help Abigail set the table,"

Samantha rolled on as she continued reading the lunch schedule.

"Good." Darla said. "Sally and Clark can take care of Shadoe. Sally, make sure Shadoe has fresh water," she directed.

"Okay Darla," agreed Sally joyously.

Sally went to the water and food dish she had so lovingly kept nearby for this very occasion. Clark followed her over waiting to be guided by her.

"Careful Clark, follow directions," Sally patiently guided him in her exuberant fashion as she reverently gave Clark the dogfood dish. "Give her two scoops of dog food for now," she said good-naturedly.

Clark was happy to comply. He went into the pantry, took the plastic lid off of a large container they had previously filled with dog food, again in anticipation of Shadoe's arrival. They had overheard the staff a few days earlier, and trying to contain this news had almost caused a rebellion. After awhile, with the dog watered and the table set, sandwiches and juice were served. Everyone sat down to a lunch with the newest member of the family and Shadoe was happy to have her first official meal in her new home. She actually laid down and ate out of her dish in a prone position . . . much to the entertainment of everyone except Samantha, who was easily able to ignore Shadoe's existence.

That afternoon, after lunch was finished and the kitchen cleaned up, everyone again reported out to the yard to finish up the weekend yard work. Tomorrow was Sunday and everyone wanted to go to a movie as Antwan had promised them from last weekend. Sally and Abigail were back to cleaning up around the dumpster, Ike patiently moved back to sweeping the patio and the sidewalks around the house. Chico and Clark were picking up dead branches around the yard in preparation for the agency's maintenance team, which came and cut the lawn as they did for all the residences managed by the agency.

Hector was more comfortable now and was able to help Darla pick up sticks and place them in a pile that the other two fellows had started. Shadoe explored her new front and back yard and her new comrades. She was happy to stay in the vicinity as it was obvious that she considered herself one of the gang.

As Darla was outside with everyone assisting them with any difficulties they may have encountered while they completed their chores, Samantha had taken the opportunity to sit in the office and do her web surfing. Usually Darla would push her to be outside and help everyone. But today she was content that Samantha was isolating herself as Shadoe bonded with everyone else in the house.

In the meantime Klupkick and his sidekick Seymour were cruising down Ferris Road for one of their frequent drive-by visits. His obsession with what he referred to as that retard house still drove him. As he slowly cruised past Ferris House Seymour was in the shotgun seat slurping on a Budweiser.

He was out on his own recognizance until trial from the previous event at the bowling alley.

"Look at those fuckin' retards. They got that mutt dog back again. That's our tax money you know, we gotta shell it out for that dog and her dog food," Klupkick spit vehemently.

Seymour rolled his eyes at his buddy again. "Why do you have to drive by this tard house all the time?" Seymour muttered. "It's Saturday afternoon, let's go to the bar and have some more brews and watch the ball game. You let them tards get to you too much."

Then Seymour brightened up because he spied Sally in the front yard.

"Look there's that Sally again. I still think she was ready to come with me but for that big jungle-bunny guy pulled me back and made it look like I did something wrong."

"You did do something wrong," Klupkick grunted out. "There's something wrong with, you wanting to make it with that stinkin' retard girl. Just go home with your computer porn," he concluded.

Seymour smiled leeringly as he contemplated his perv' thoughts.

"What the hell you gonna' do if you get her knocked-up. She'd only have a retard and then there's more people we gotta take care of with our tax money. All that retards can have is more retards. They should sterilize them, don't let them breed," Klupkick finished profoundly.

He was pleased with this chain of reasoning. By then, they had passed the house and came up to a stop sign at the end of the road.

"Make a right and head towards the Hazard Inn," Seymour suggested.

The truck's tailgate thankfully disappeared into the distance.

As this transpired Joan was laboring in her rose garden next door to Ferris House. Marc was in the pole barn working on his tractor. She noticed Klupkick's truck go by again as she loosened the dirt around her cherished roses. She considered that this had become a regular occurrence this summer since the new neighbors had moved in next door.

She gazed some distance over into her new neighbor's yard and considered. "*Oh they have that dog back, that's nice. Any family needs a good dog,*" she pondered. She thought of their old dog Bear and how she missed him. "*Maybe it's time to get another one,*" she considered. "*That way the dog next door will have a playmate.*"

She put down her shovel, took off her garden gloves and walked back to the pole barn, where Marc was under the tractor getting dirty again and cursing in a low voice.

"Dear are you busy?" she inquired sweetly.

"Of course not Joan I'm just lying under this tractor here taking a nap," Marc grumbled sarcastically.

"Don't be a smart ass dear," Joan stated ominously.

"But that's what I'm best at lammy pie, taking naps under tractors and being a smart ass."

Joan ignored this smart-alecky comment out of habit.

"I've been thinking."

"Oh shit," Marc mumbled to himself. "Not again."

"I heard that."

"I'm sure you did sweetie. What are you thinking about?" he inquired, feigning interest.

"I think we should get another dog. I miss Bear. I think we need a puppy, maybe a nice Black Lab," Joan put her index finger on her chin thoughtfully.

"Shit."

Marc slid out from under the tractor. Bear was his dog. It was hard when he died. It's always hard when good people lose a member of the family and for people like Marc and Joan Ferris any beast or person that came into their house by definition was a member of the family.

Marc looked her square in the eye, saw that look in his wife's beautiful blue eyes and realized right away where this conversation was going. For a split-second he considered. Then he realized he would like another dog too.

"Maybe that's a good idea," he stated pointedly to Joan, "I think the Adams' on the other side of the county still have some good dogs, but theirs are Plot Hounds. He takes them up state to run the bears out of cornfields."

Joan liked the progress she was making with her husband.

"Okay dear, we'll talk about it. I don't know if Plot hounds are good. They have to run a lot, but I guess so do Black Labs," she thought out loud.

"Black Labs?" Marc questioned. "We'll talk about the idea after dinner," he finished, or so he thought. Marc went to climb back under the tractor and was stopped by that look of contemplation on Joan's face. "Is there something more?" he questioned.

"Now that you mention it, there is, my dear husband."

"Oh shit, now what?" Marc complained with mild impatience.

"Where did you get such a naughty mouth?" Joan chided in a cautioning tone.

"From hanging around with you dear, please go on. What else were you considering? I know I can't get any work done until you have all this off your gorgeous chest," he smiled expectantly.

She threw the gloves she was holding at his face. He ducked and quickly advanced to a point directly in front of her. She screamed and tried to run, giggling like a schoolgirl. They were like two teenagers again. He grabbed her and spun her around; hugging her around the waist he tried to kiss her neck. She beat on his back playfully with her fists.

"Not now, if you're good maybe later," she taunted.

"You'll do as I say, woman."

"You'll do as I say if you want to get lucky," she laughed.

They kissed. He gazed into her eyes.

"Oh yeah, I almost forgot one more thing," she said.

He inhaled almost fearfully. "What is it this time?"

"I think we should invite our new neighbors to a cookout, it's the neighborly thing to do," Joan smiled happily.

"You got to be kidding me," Marc declared.

"No I'm not." She looked at him reproachfully. "It's the Christian thing to do."

Remembering his days as an employee at the local psych center several considerations simultaneously occurred to Marc. "*I better check the carpet cleaner to see if it still works,*" he thought. He dared not say this out loud as he knew she would get angry at him.

"Sure, why not?" Marc smiled jovially, "what can it hurt, they might like some good food for a change."

thinking fast. "We can have it outside on the patio; we'll pick a nice sunny day, I'll let you give them the invitation dear. You have a real talent for bringing way-wards into our house to invade our privacy," he smiled. She slapped him playfully across his face. He grabbed her forcefully in his strong arms so she couldn't get away this time. They kissed again, and he released her.

"Just give me some early warning, so I can clean the grill and pull some fresh vegetables out of the stand … make sure my shotguns put away … lock up the good silver," he trailed off as he crawled back under the tractor. Joan was already thinking of other things as she walked back out of the pole barn and returned to her garden, feeling good about what they discussed.

"A new dog," she thought to herself. *"We could use one. I'm curious about that one tall Asian fellow; we'll see what he's like up close. Seems like he just wants some friends, who knows how hard his life has been,"* she mulled this over as an afterthought.

She then remembered she forgot to tell Marc about Klupkick making a habit to drive by the house. She noticed this became more frequent just recently. She soon forgot about that also as she got back to her garden. She became lost in admiring her roses and caring for them in her usual intense fashion. She was already trying to think of a name for the new dog.

"Maybe we'll get two dogs," she thought; she then became lost in the fragrant allure of her garden.

"Computers, I hate them," Elmer thought .

He sat in front of the computer in the office. The phone rang.

"Ferris House," Elmer answered .

He forlornly answered the phone. He listened for a moment. It was the I.T. guy from Disabled People of Americas' campus.

"Yeah, Bob you know how careful we are with this thing, everything is updated, but it's still acting funny. Strange things keep popping up. Sites I know that nobody could've gone to. Believe me I've never seen some of the positions these naked people are in."

Elmer listened to the caller for a moment. “Okay half an hour, I'll be here, thanks goodbye.”

Elmer stared at the computer. **Geek girls in your area for fun and games … Free sex with the woman of your fantasies,** promised the computer monitor.

“I hate computers,” Elmer thought to himself again. “Darla,” he called, “come in here please.”

It was Wednesday, and all the residents of Ferris House were either at work and or at program. Elmer was hoping to catch up on all the house paperwork that had been neglected since last Friday. Darla came into the office from the kitchen. She looked at the computer screen.

“You know, you really shouldn't go to those sites; you could lose your job if the higher-ups found out,” she accused with mock seriousness.

Elmer gave her an evil glare. Darla couldn't help but twist the knife a little deeper.

“You know, if you're lonely I have some girlfriends you might like to meet instead of this cyber stuff you seem to be enjoying so much,” she suggested.

“Alright, alright,” Elmer grumbled. “That's enough of that.”

“Just trying to help boss,” Darla smiled devilishly down to him.

Elmer ignored this. “We’ve got to have a meeting. We all have to sit down and talk about this computer. I don't know how this stuff got here. But this is a real problem, especially with all the safeguards we have on this machine. This stuff can only be coming in if someone is going to the wrong sites or is opening the wrong e-mails.”

Darla became more serious. “I know what you mean. We have a staff meeting coming up next week; we will go over it with everyone then. But I think I have an idea who this could be.”

“I know, it's probably Samantha,” Elmer answered unhappily. “She likes to surf those ‘have a psychic dinner with your new soul mate’ websites. Who knows what kind of crap comes in from there?”

He looked up at Darla and waved his hand at the computer monitor. “We have to have a computer. Maybe we'll have to put a password on the Internet access. After all, Chico only e-mails on it when someone else is around. So we know it's not him. Plus, by checking the history of those dates, they don't match up from some of the sites that were visited on the days that Chico was using the computer to e-mail his friend anyway."

"Having all the forms on the computer sure saves us a lot of handwriting, and a lot of time," Darla added as an afterthought.

"I know it does," Elmer admitted. "I like it too when it's working right. Everyone has computers. You can't compete in the world without one. All this modern technology, it's great when it works, otherwise it's a pain in the ass."

He had his chin on his fist, his elbow on the desk staring miserably at the computer.

"Well, one good thing," Darla resumed. "Thank God none of the residents were around to see this; we wouldn't want to open that can of worms." Changing gears, Darla asked. "So what do you think about our neighbors inviting us over for a cookout?"

"I was surprised," Elmer began. "But it's good to see. At least we know not everybody hates us around here, we just have to make sure everyone's on their best behavior. So far, everyone has adjusted quite well, but they will have to work on table manners. And I don't just mean the residents. But then again if the neighbors invited us they must have some idea of what they're getting into. It looks like we're set for weekend after next on a Sunday afternoon. Joan Ferris and her husband Marc have been around a long time. They're good people to have on our side in the community, not that anyone can force us out at this point. But it's always better if the neighbors are our friends. Then they can find out for themselves that we're more alike than they might realize."

"Thank you, Father Elmer," Darla ribbed. "I have to get back to work before everyone gets home this afternoon. I have to shampoo the carpets upstairs. I just have to keep the fans running on them. Between that and the air-conditioning they should be dry by tonight, when everyone's ready to go start messing them up again," Darla commented as she walked out of the office.

As Darla departed, Elmer sat staring at the monitor. **'Free sex in your town tonight,'** it happily announced to him. "I hate computers," Elmer said to the empty room …

Later on that night, two miles away, at the end of a dead-end street (by the way, this was not one of the best areas, more like tobacco road), there sat a rundown bungalow. In the driveway of this little palace, which had been converted years before the advent of modern codes, there sat the same black truck that had been observed frequenting the area around Ferris House.

Along with the truck there was an old rusted LTD II as well as other recognizable and unrecognizable debris strewn about the yard. A rotten pile of split wood, an old toilet, a refrigerator with the door off, and an old dog kennel with rusted, sagging, chain-link walls.

That dog kennel, although it hadn't been used in some time, still looked as though it was filthy with petrified piles of dog feces from some long-ago forlorn neglected beast.

Travel down a well worn dirt path strewn with litter on both sides, through drab unremarkable water stained doors; go into a filthy house smelling of old musty goodness knew what. Also cluttered with more inarticulate odds and ends, and eureka: home sweet home.

That there were only pathways through the years of clutter going from room to room as access was more evidence of excessive slothfulness. The bungalow contained a tiny kitchen, a living room, a bedroom, and a bathroom. In the bedroom sat Jay Klupkick, intently dallying in front of his computer.

He had claimed disability for many years and had just enough money for gas, food, and his car payment. He had no mortgage on the bungalow. He had acquired it from beating the one live-in girlfriend he had had so badly, that she sold it to him for a song. Then she fled to California to put as much distance between Klupkick and herself as she possibly could without leaving the 48 states.

Apparently he also was able to afford a used and abused computer with dial-up, for his continued entertainment. Klupkick sat in a chair in front of his computer surfing some of the more disgusting pornographic sites. He had way too much time on his hands. He mumbled to himself as he surfed and did what came naturally.

Most people in polite society would be nauseated even to consider the graphic nature of this man's life. He was truly was what some would call a waste of life. The only redeeming factor for him was somewhere he must have had a mother that once loved him.

One time when he was very young, about 12 years old, his drunken father had laid hands on Klupkick's mother yet again with the usual result. That was the first time and last time that Klupkick tried to do anything remotely noble. He paid the same price that all paid in that house of anguish. He never tried to step up for anyone again. Although his mother loved her husband and family, both the mother and father were drunks; she took the abuse as many did in similar situations and was never able to break the cycle. Being functional alcoholics they could hold down jobs, usually pay their bills, and —and, well that was about it.

Klupkick had had an older sister, but she ran away as soon as she was 15 years old. No one ever heard from her again, everyone in the house knew why, but no one spoke of the kind of man Klupkick's father was or his vile habits.

Maybe there was a peculiarity in Klupkick's brain. But when his father would beat his mother in a drunken rage, Klupkick bought in to the statements made by his father, that she deserved it, that he had a right as the husband to physically abuse his wife. And use her any way he deemed appropriate. These were moralistic values that Klupkick carried with him throughout his life.

He was a portly young fellow and by the time he dropped out of school he was a well known bully and coward. He remained a bully (and coward) throughout his pitiful life.

Klupkick additionally, even to this day, could still be a proven coward when confronted. He would back off, and even became frightened of someone that was strong enough to stand against him and tell him 'no', you can't brutalize people. This sort of event, when it took place, made Klupkick even angrier. But if by chance he perceived the target to be physically weaker and obviously vulnerable to his intimidation, well then, the bully throve.

So when any opportunity did present itself he would take out this anger on the weaker and more defenseless around him with great satisfaction. Any of the fairer gender he was lucky enough to charm would make themselves scarce—quick-like-a-bunny when his brutality emerged.

He had put women in the hospital before who had been weak enough to stay around too long.

Most people that tried to befriend Klupkick learned in short order that he was despicable and a repudiation of anything humane or even remotely civilized. Except for his drunken friend Seymour, who was co-dependent on manifest abuse from his own upbringing, and had adjusted well to the degradation from Klupkick.

Klupkick had dropped Seymour off earlier and then proceeded to his hovel for his usual evening fare. He didn't care if he had good food, only that he had a lot of it. He was a good-sized man with large powerful arms, but he carried a lot of this weight in his belly.

As he sat in his chair in front of his barely serviceable computer and impatiently waited for his perverse images to download, Klupkick actually muttered to himself.

"Fuckin' retards, the Nazis had the right idea keepin' them in institutions. They're useless to work. Just put them down bad dogs. Ain't right someone like me has put up with that crap… in my town, of all places, keep them down in the city, with them bleeding hearts. It ain't enough to have them Communist Buddhists moved in here some years back with all their chanting and crap. This ain't the U.S. of A. no more. It's turned into some fag la-te-da Euro-shit country."

Klupkick could picture that dog in his head running happily that afternoon at the Ferris House, and all the little gimp window- lickers working around the yard and playing with that split-tail bitch mutt, like they had a right to.

Klupkick had a real anger/rage problem. Actually it was uncontrollable fury, and when this took over violence always ensued. Where he knew that he was the strongest among the weak he always lashed out with fierce coercion. Klupkick squashed his beer can—**squish,** against the wall within easy reach in front of him.

"Them damn split-tails, I'll get them," he vowed.

The red anger in his gaze began to clear as he looked at the perverse images which began to materialize on his computer. This gradually drained away his ferocity and he sat mesmerized by the debasing image of a woman in bondage being beaten, as well as other unmentionable debasements being committed against her person. His more primitive instincts took over and

Klupkick was taken into his world of perversion and pleasure … outside of his pathetic existence for a short while.

One lone streetlight came on down at the end of the road. Nearby the neighbors could heard Klupkick rant viciously. They were glad that this night he had become silent earlier than usual, fortunately a brief release from the dread they experienced daily, living in such close proximity to someone possessed with so much malevolence …

9
Justice for All
(Sometimes the system actually works)

As the town that contained Ferris House was only a small village, the civil servants and elected officials were all part-timers. The judge, Judge John Frick, had been a career man in a state trooper barracks. After he retired he campaigned and was easily elected as the local judge. He was also from the area, and had lived here all his life, except when he had to travel to other parts of the state throughout his career as a trooper. He knew the local lay of the land, he knew who was who and what was what; he had been a judge going on five years now.

He started as a state trooper when he was 21 years old, worked 29 years and was able to retire. He was 55 now, but still lean with sinewy strength and a flat belly. He liked to take care of himself, and he liked to take care of the town he lived in. He held court once a week during the day and once a week in the evening. Usually his court consisted of traffic tickets and local kids that got into some trouble, the usual teenage stuff. But things had been changing lately in the area. Drugs were moving in, bad drugs and even some gangs. He knew this from his friends at the barracks, and also because of some of the issues that came across his bench. He hated to see this happen as much as the next person did in a quiet town.

Tonight, he had a case come before him with Seymour Hinkel. He knew about Seymour, not a real bright fella, and a heavy drinker, prone to finding trouble without even realizing that he was getting into it.

Judge John was just buttoning up his black robe when Janie, a fifty something year old blond with her hair perpetually pulled back into a tight bun, his court clerk, poked her head into his chambers.

"We got a full house tonight Your Honor."

"Yeah," he nodded to Janie. "I'm ready, want to go announce me? I'm coming right behind you."

Janie retreated back out the door, to the small courtroom. She nodded to Police Chief Pete Anderson. Chief Anderson intoned solemnly ‘all rise’ for his honorable Judge John Frick. An assortment of people present in the courtroom struggled to their feet and stood there quietly until the judge entered and seated himself. Again Police Chief Anderson stated in his baritone. ‘Please be seated’ and the crowd obediently complied.

Janie handed Judge John the first folder on the docket. The judge patiently eyeballed the folder without looking at the courtroom full of people. He was silently pleased that Seymour’s case was the first one on the docket tonight. Already knowing the answer, Judge John looked up.

“Is there a Seymour Hinkel here?” he asked.

Seymour silently stood up with his lawyer supplied from the county, Attorney Ray Johnson.

“Please be seated,” Judge John stated. “Is there a legal representative for the Disabled People of America, Inc. present in the courtroom?”

Three men and a young woman stood up for Judge John to recognize. One had been there before. He was the attorney that handled the purchase of the local house on Ferris Road for the agency when they moved to the village last fall. The other one he knew to be the Executive Director of the agency, but the third one and the young woman he did not know.

“Please state your names for the court,” the judge commanded.

The attorney for the agency, a tall fellow with a lot of forehead and glasses spoke first. “I'm Attorney Jimmy Johns, representing the Disabled People of America, Inc.”

The Executive Director, a tall man with a mop of reddish gray hair, was beside him. “Your Honor, I am Robert Powers, Executive Director for Disabled People of America, Inc,” he stated.

Then the third man, not quite as relaxed as the others, spoke. “Your Honor I’m Elmer Palmer, Residential Manager for Ferris Road residence.” Elmer put his hand on Sally’s shoulder to encourage her to speak, but Sally was frozen with trepidation.

Judge John rolled on. “I presume this young lady next to you is Sally Stanton?” Judge John nodded his head toward Sally.

Elmer gave Sally's shoulder a gentle squeeze and gently whispered to her.

"Yes s-sir that's me, I'm Sally," she sputtered out.

Judge John smiled for the first time since court was brought to order.

"That's fine, young lady you have no reason to be nervous, now please everyone be seated so we can continue. We already had a hearing of the charges against Seymour Hinkel last week. Due to the sensitive nature of the charges and the individuals involved in this case. I will put the court in recess for 15 minutes. I would ask all parties if they would retire to my chambers, and we'll see where this thing's going." **Bang** went the gavel.

"All rise," Chief Anderson stated. "The court will be in recess for 15 minutes."

Small groans arose from those that did not want to be there, probably with minor traffic tickets and such. Some wondered how long this would take, Judge John was known for not rushing through things. The judge had already disappeared through the door behind his desk as the others were being ushered to a side door where they could meet in Judge John's chambers.

The inside of Judge's chambers was like that of any other small office in a small municipal building. The judge was already seated at his desk in a relaxed manner.

"Gentlemen and young lady please sit down and let's run through this," Judge John said.

Police Chief Anderson was standing with his back to the door. Judge John looked at Seymour.

"You know you're in a lot of trouble on this one Mr. Hinkel, a lot of trouble," the judge stated ominously.

Seymour started to speak. His attorney put his hand on his arm and shushes him down.

"That's right," Judge John said . "Never interrupt his honor, makes him cranky you know. You can actually get some prison time on this one Mr. Hinkel. I've already discussed this with the Executive Director of Disabled People of America, Inc. and their attorneys, who by the way have discussed it with the individual involved and of course your attorney. If you change your plea to guilty I'll sentence you to 90 days in the county jail and five years probation. And after you get out I'll sign an order of protection for you to stay away from the individuals at Ferris House.

Also, you're fortunate that they are such understanding members of the community and by the very nature of their business, their philosophy leans toward rehabilitation. At this time, would you like to discuss this with your attorney?" Judge John intoned severely.

Seymour never was one to confront authority on a scale such as this. The worst he had ever confronted was that one time with his mother and the prom incident. Look what that got him. Even though he continued to believe he had done nothing wrong to Sally and she was still fair game, past experiences had shown him that it's better to tell people what they want to hear, and ninty days ain't bad. He'd been there before; he shuffled his feet and glanced at his public defender, looking down he knew the best act was sheepishness.

"Yes, judge," he stated quietly. "I would like to change my plea to guilty."

"Excellent," Judge John replied, delighted. "I just love it when everyone gets along. OK, gentlemen, you can proceed back out to the courtroom where we can make the disposition of this case official." The judge looked past everyone to Chief Anderson and spoke. "Would you please show everyone back to the courtroom," he declared cheerfully, "I have lots of speeding tickets to punish. Good evening gentlemen."

Judge John looked intently at Sally. "And welcome to the community young lady. You're in a nice area with good neighbors. Hopefully things will run much smoother for you in the future."

Sally was still somewhat intimidated by his authority and demeanor; she smiled sheepishly. "Thank you judge," she said, her natural gentleness emerging.

The Executive Director for Disabled People of America, Inc. and their attorney allowed Elmer to usher Sally out of the office first, then followed after them. Seymour and his public defender also proceeded to the courtroom proper. All Elmer could think to himself as he walked out of the judge's office just behind Sally was that hopefully things will settle down for awhile. After all, this was probably the worst of it anyway.

And for a while, at Ferris House, things did seem to settle into greased grooves. Hector and Ike seemed to find a way to deal with the inequities that confronted them at program. Abigail and Sally seemingly did the same.

Maybe the people that misunderstood them were just too preoccupied with their own lives to expend the energy confronting them for the trivial idiosyncrasies that anyone might possess. Maybe some of these people were no longer working at these places also, like Fred.

For whatever reason, things were almost too easy to be believed. Chico was doing well at his job handing out food samples at the local shopping center. Clark, as shy and introverted as ever, seemed to take a special interest in making sure that Shadoe's dog bed was clean, her food and water dishes were also clean and that her toys were all piled up where she seemed to like them best.

Shadoe had really taken to being a member of the family at Ferris House. If anyone scrutinized her closely, they would notice that she watched the individuals that lived there very closely. If someone didn't come for dinner on time she went to look for them. As soon as she came in from outside Shadoe liked to check every room in the house.

Darla had commented that this was the standard neurotic behavior of a well bred German Shepherd Dog even if Shadoe was was a mutt. It even got to the point that if Chico, the girls, Clark or anyone else were cleaning up sticks, Shadoe would actually grab some sticks in her mouth and drag them over to the pile with everyone else. One Saturday afternoon before the landscape crew came from campus to cut the lawn, Darla observed Shadoe doing this.

Even Hector settled down. He did not seem to be slapping his head as much or screaming with trepidation. He seemed to be content to stay in his space at the edge of the yard. And he even came over and assisted the rest of his ad-hoc family in their menial tasks of caring for their new home. Yes, events truly seemed to be entering a golden age for everyone at Ferris House.

Even Samantha had settled down, and for all intents and purposes, seemed less harmful to those for whom she was theoretically there to care for. She spent more time with the people at Ferris House assisting them with their tasks, or at least not hindering them.

Maybe the password block that was put on the Internet access helped her concentrate more on her job and less on her

Internet surfing. Still, she was very smart and did try to weasel the password out of those who knew it, but to no avail. Antwan and the other employees at the house including the night crew came in and did their jobs in practical fashion. The paperwork was done. The programs were completed. Inspections were made by the higher-ups. Surely this was another another shining success story for Disabled People of America, Inc. in mainstreaming people with disabilities into the community.

And so as the days went by, the people that lived at Ferris House became excited. Some of the employees that worked there were also excited. The big cookout at the neighbors' house, Marc and Joan, was approaching that weekend.

The exalted weekend finally arrived. Sunday, after all the chores were completed, both families would meet in the backyard on the patio next door. Marc Ferris and Joan Ferris would welcome their new neighbors to break bread.

A few other guests from the neighborhood had also been invited to attend. The Adams', the people from across town that had given Marc and Joan the new dog, a Black Lab as it turned out, would be there.

The new dog, Buddy as he was named, had become great pals with Shadoe. Shadoe and Buddy loved to play and frolic together as doggy friends did and everyone enjoyed their antics.

Also on the guest list was Martha and her husband Josh who worked Marc's vegetable stand part time in the summer. They were coming with their two children, little Josh and little Moe, a couple of terrors. And Benito and his wife Gladys would be in attendance. Benito helped Marc part time farming the fields; they rounded out the line-up that was to dine with the Ferris House gang. In all it would be quite a crowd.

The people who lived at Ferris House were very keyed up. Even some of the employees were pleased to be attending. It broke the monotony of work and they wanted to enjoy a good time as well. The other staff fortunately had the day off, or were at least able to be tolerant enough to do what must be done for the get-together to be a success, even if they would rather be somewhere else.

This morning Darla was a little more poignant than usual with her fellow employees. That Nunzia was present with Her, 'I'm only here for my own pleasure and the money' attitude, didn't go far this morning. She truly enjoyed antagonizing Darla with her little jibes. But Darla did better than to let this get to her.

Antwan was present, ready to enjoy the day in his usual laid-back style. He simply let Darla and Nunzia do their verbal fencing and got on with the business at hand.

Clark detected the tension between Darla and Nunzia like radar, but was able to keep his anxiety to a minimum. Chico, Hector, and Ike milled around, excited to be going to meet the neighbors up close.

Darla was checking to see that all was in order, that they had their t-shirts on right side out, and they didn't have any tears or stains on them, then went on to check the desserts that Sally and Abigail had assisted her in making the day before. Nunzia obediently wrapped up a bowl of potato salad that she was kind enough to make and bring in to show that she wasn't all bad and could be a joiner when she had to be. But inevitably the sarcasm was there.

"So Darla, how long do you think it will be before someone starts eating the potato salad with their hands in front of neighbors?"

Darla answered her sweetly. "That depends on how hungry you get Nunzia."

Nunzia simmered at leaving an opening for such an obvious retort, apparently not on her usual game.

Antwan chuckled in the corner and continued to quiz the gentlemen. "Ike, your shirt is not buttoned up right. You missed a button."

"I'mm sorrry Antwan," Ike stated in his usual lackadaisical drawl.

"That's all right. Why don't let me help you with that," Antwan offered kindly.

"Shadoe can come with us, right?" Clark dipped his head down and asked for the umpteenth time.

"Yes," Antwan answered automatically again for the umpteenth time, seemingly never to run short of patience. "Of course she can. She wants to see her friend Buddy and I know she wants to have some of that good food too."

Clark was again reassured for a short time.

Hector calmly rocked back and forth with a happy little smile on his face. Almost with his eyes closed as though he were meditating, more at peace with the world around him than some people deserved to be.

Chico was excited also and started with questions. “Will we have cheeseburgers there Darla?”

“You know we're going to have cheeseburgers there,” Darla acknowledged.

“Can I have onions on mine?” Chico inquired.

Antwan smiled at him. “Is that all you think about Chico?”

“Look, old man,” Chico grinned happily at Antwan. “I-I-I know you want a cheeseburger too.”

Antwan smiled at him. “You’re right there, at least one, I wouldn’t miss it for the world.”

It was going on 11:30 in the morning and Nunzia was passing out the medications for everyone. “Alright you guys, when I call your name come over to the medication closet. One at a time, no confusion, I don't want another medication error.”

“You can't afford another one,” Darla jabbed.

Nunzia silently mimicked Darla as she made an exaggerated face at her from beside the medication closet door.

Darla smiled back at her wide eyed and affable.

“Alright Chico, you first,” Nunzia announced.

Chico immediately went over and took the proffered cup with medication. He made an odd face as he always did and put the pills in his hand and then up to his eyes and looked closely at them to make sure they were the proper ones. He obediently took the water from Nunzia’s outstretched hand. After checking his pills again he swallowed them down.

Next was Clark. He asked the same question he always did. “Is this the right pill?” he cocked his head and stuttered out. This was something Clark had recently begun to do. Especially since he was told that he didn’t have to take his pill if he didn’t want to. But he also was afraid not to take it. That he continually questioned now made him feel as though he had some control. As this was one of the first times in his life he actually had some control, Clark asked every time.

“Clark, you ask me that question every time,” Nunzia declared in a bored fashion.

"And he has a right to ask that question every time," Darla happily confirmed, again taking the opportunity to rebut Nunzia.

Anyone present could sense this ongoing competition between the two which was not going to abate anytime soon. Clark took his pill and slunk away like a whipped puppy, which was in character for him even in his most assertive of times.

Darla's heart went out to Clark. "Come over and help me with Shadoe. I want to make sure her collar's on right," she said.

If Clark were a dog he would have wagged his tail and given a great big doggie smile to Darla. Anything to do with Shadoe brightened his very being. He had so little to lighten his days in his short 45 years that an event like Shadoe coming into it had changed everything for him.

Through this mild emotional brush fire Elmer had been in the office listening to the preparations that the employees and residents had been making at Ferris House. It was almost show time. Elmer's stomach always got butterflies at this point, when he had to go to a strange place with his charges. He knew a lot of people would be at the picnic, and he didn't know how things would go. People were always so unpredictable. And not simply the people that he served at Disabled People of America, Inc.

As the events outside of his office built to a crescendo, Elmer felt it was time. He calmly looked down at both of his hands on the desk blotter, took a deep breath and resigned himself to whatever was going to happen that afternoon. He let out a long breath, stood up and calmly put the chair under the desk and went out into the kitchen.

Immediately, Hector ran over and grabbed his hand. He knew Hector enjoyed his company on some level, but never quite understood what was going through Hector's mind. Individuals afflicted with autism had difficulty forming friendships. Elmer considered it impossible to fathom some of Hector's motivations.

"Alright everyone," intoned Elmer in his best I'm 'the chief' voice. "Is everyone ready? Are we going to have fun when we meet our new neighbors?"

Clark looked down at his feet and ducked his head in his usual fashion.

Chico smiled happily like the innocent soul that he was. “You bet I am Elmer, I-I-I hope we have a cheeseburger,” he said.

Antwan smiled down at Chico and intoned in his deliciously baritone voice, “You know we will, Chico.”

“I'm ready to have a lot of fun today,” Sally put in. “Our neighbor Joan said it'll be a pleasure to have some other ladies in the house for a change; she told me that when she came over to invite us.” Sally smiled happily at Elmer. She tried to sound nonchalant and not as nervous as she felt, and almost succeeded on some level. Nunzia was almost going to taunt her but thought better of it as Elmer was present. They were going to be together for the afternoon and she knew she had to be on her best behavior.

Shadoe happily wagged her tail as she stood beside Clark patiently waiting like the rest. Darla and Nunzia both gave a mocking smile to Elmer, Darla’s good natured and Nunzia’s in her usual cynical bent.

Elmer walked over to Nunzia and intoned in a little voice next to her ear. “You behave yourself over there; I know what you can do.”

Nunzia put on a mock hurt face. “Boss you know I only have the best interests of the house and the people that we serve at heart.”

“Yeah,” Elmer mumbled as he continued past her to the door. “Alright let’s put on our best we belong here faces.”

Smiling at Nunzia, he grabbed the door handle and with a flourish, opened the door and held it open standing to one side.

“Lead the way Darla; he gestured with his free hand, let's put our best foot forward.”

They all trailed happily out of the house, Shadoe pranced alongside just as excited as the rest of Ferris House, as if she knew she was going to see her pal Buddy.

They walked out of the back door, across the blacktop, and past the dumpster in a line like a caravan carrying their wares from a far off land, trekking over the property line into the backyard where Joan Ferris was waiting. She smiled at the group and faced Elmer.

"It certainly is a delight you could bring everyone. Please come over to the tables and sit down and relax so we can begin the festivities of the afternoon," she finished kindly.

Marc was standing there with Joan, and their new Black Lab, Buddy. The brief moment of tension that happened when new people met happened, and was quickly swept away. Shadoe happily ran over and started frolicking with Buddy and any of the uncomfortableness quickly vanished while the innocent beasts took it away with their good natured comportment.

Sally smiled and squealed with delight at the antics of the dogs. Joan couldn't help but laugh and clapped her hands together; Marc, her husband, relaxed and greeted Elmer with a good manly handshake and a slap on the shoulder.

"Good to have you, neighbor," Marc smiled amiably.

"Thank's for having us, Marc. This is truly a pleasure," Elmer returned as he shook Marc's hand.

Taking a chance at levity Elmer continued, "Are you sure you won't be 'branded people' in the neighborhood now for having us over?"

Marc relaxed even more and gave an easy laugh.

"We've been marked people in this neighborhood for generations. We never let that stop us from visiting our neighbors or dealing with good people. For that matter, just to give you a heads up, the wife used to work in a psych center... I did too. We enjoy helping people, used to volunteer, even on our days off. Things have changed a lot since then, and it's good to see people that really need help, getting it. Is there anything special we need to help you with for today?" Marc asked, finishing in a kindly fashion.

Elmer was used to this type of demeanor when dealing with people who, without even realizing it, still leaned on some of the stereotypes of previous times. But he didn't hold this against anyone, as Elmer knew, just like he told his employees time and again over the years in those wonderful monthly house meetings, either at the houses he had worked in, or in any of classes he taught for new staff.

Elmer's philosophy, nobody knows everything, and when you start to think you do, you stop learning. We're here to teach. This he would impress upon any individual or group unlucky enough to be present when he began to pontificate. He smiled at Marc, starting the usual delicate education of the second part of his philosophy, which happens to be, the more disabled people can do for themselves, just like regular people, the better off everyone was.

"Actually, maybe we can help you. Everyone here is just like any family. They're good at some stuff and not so good at other stuff. Darla and Nunzia will help our makeshift family assist you in any way possible. I'd be happy to help you cook, and as it looks like it's going to be a real party I brought some near beer for some of the people, and as I am on duty that's all I can have. You, sir, are welcome to have the adult beverage of your choice; in the meantime, please don't let our presence stop you," Elmer finished.

Marc was already occupied as he endeavored to sort through the gear for the barbeque.

"Suit yourself," Marc replied kindly.

Their conversation turned to more gender-based matters, Sally, Nunzia, Darla, and Abigail gravitated toward Joan. Darla, in her easy manner, put them to work helping to set up the table and arrange the chairs.

"So, Joan," Darla began. "Thanks for having us over. Don't be afraid to put us to work," she smiled genuinely at Joan.

Nunzia chimed in with her fake enthusiasm. "Oh, we love to work," her usual smart ass self.

Joan immediately sensed the rivalry between these two, since she had worked with people like these over the years at the psych center. She already picked Darla out as a reasonable person and branded Nunzia on the nose, as someone with a slight superiority attitude at best, and she knew just what to do. "That's good;" she smiled easily to both ladies, "we're pretty much set up. Looks like you all brought a lot of good stuff over here. Let's get it laid out proper." Joan took the bowl from Nunzia. "Thank you," she smiled too sweetly.

She casually let some blue fire flow into her eyes as she locked her gaze onto Nunzia's. This way Joan let her know not to try to take advantage in her house. Nunzia was no dullard and caught on quickly, backing down for the time being. Darla caught this as only women could and liked Joan's manner instantly.

Hector shyly hovered on the outskirts of the small group; he had never been this close to the lady with auburn hair. He rocked gently back and forth with a little smile on his face. He felt good just to be near her. He had that same feeling of when he could sense gentle people around him in the old days, back at the institution.

Hector enjoyed this relaxed and easy manner as they set food out on the table and Darla guided Abigail, Sally, and Chico through the same thing they did so many times in their own backyard or at the dining room table.

Clark and Ike gravitated over towards Marc and Elmer, who were near the brick barbecue pit with a metal grill on top of it. Marc had finished setting up and was ready to go.

Marc turned toward Ike and Clark. “Hey fellas,” he started amicably. “Good to have you over, hope you brought your appetite today?”

Ike smiled and rubbed his hands together in delight. In his slow drawling speech he rolled out the magic words, “I suurre did cooome hungry.”

Clark ducked his head in a more submissive fashion and looked at Marc sideways, afraid to look him directly in the face. “H-H-Hi,” he stuttered out finally.

Marc smiled and gave a little wave to Clark and offered him a beverage, which Clark hesitantly accepted.

Elmer lay back and let the psychodynamics take root and work with Marc as well as the others.

Marc smiled kindly at Clark. “What’s your name?” he inquired.

“My name's C-C-Clark.”

Clark tried to calm down a little. He wanted to be accepted by this person.

“Clark,” Marc said. “Did you know your name means scholar?” inquired Marc, trying to put Clark more at ease with small talk.

“Yeah, yeah,” Clark said. “I knew that.” Clark was surprised that someone else would know that.

“We don’t need to be shy,” you’re our neighbors and we’re happy to have you,” Marc assured him.

Kindly, matter-of-factly, still trying to set Clark at ease, Marc continued. “Clark, you guys do a good job keeping your yard nice over there. That's a lot of work; it's a big place.”

“Yeah … yeah, a lot of work,” Clark said.

Warming up a little bit more, not knowing what to say, Clark continued to fidget uncertainly. He gravitated toward the one thing he knew well, TV from the 60s and 70s; shows like the ones he used to watch back on Ward 23 in the institution as a young man.

"The Brady Bunch, I watch the Brady Bunch," Clark ventured, attempting to make conservation.

Meanwhile, Ike was staring at the food on the side of the grill ready to go on the fire; he was mesmerized. "Brady Bunch," Ike parroted absentmindedly.

He was simply repeating what he heard like a recorder as he concentrated on the food.

"No more, not the Brady Bunch." Ike put into the conversation in a nonsensical way.

Marc picked up a spatula and looked at Elmer, who was standing there quietly observing the other two men. Elmer cut in to try to make the conversation more comfortable. "I'm an Addams Family man myself," he said.

"Addams Family," Ike repeated.

It was obvious that he was not truly paying attention to the conversation.

Just then the Adams family arrived: John, not Gomez, the one that gave the Ferris' their new dog, Buddy. Mr. Adams walked up to the group.

"Mention my name, Marc?" he asked.

"Not unless you're Gomez; we're talking about old TV shows," Marc said.

John Adams caught on fast. "I'm a Munster's man myself; myself; oh, that Lilly M., what a gal."

"They're funny," Ike stated as he watched the grill like a hawk. "I want a cheeseburger."

"Now Ike, be more polite, say please," Elmer cut in.

Marc caught on fast. "That's the magic word around here. You can get anything you want with the please word."

"Pleeaase?" Ike drawled out slowly. "I'd like a to have a cheeseburger."

Needless to say Marc smiled at this, beginning to recall the pleasures of helping others, especially those less fortunate than he was. As he started making burgers to put on the fire he made more light conversation.

"You strike me as fellows that are always hungry. Nothing wrong with that," he continued. "Hard work makes a man hungry. You have to feed the machine," he finished in a comfortable fashion.

"Feed the machine," Ike repeated absentmindedly.

Clark was still shy but warming up fast.

"The Munster's, they—they were a scary program. They were scary, that dragon, Spot. He made me nervous. He gave me nightmares," Clark said in earnest.

Marc began to put more food on the grill and took off the first of the burgers. "Just about ready, hope you guys are hungry," he repeated again.

"Can we help you with any of that?" John Adams asked.

"Well you can spell me when the time comes, but for now you can take some orders if you would," Marc requested.

By then the other guests had begun to arrive.

"Clark, if you would stay with me, there is some near beer that you guys brought. You can put it on ice. There's the ice chest over there with ice in it," Marc said , hoping to get Clark involved.

Clark glanced cryptically at Marc as John and Elmer walked away to take requests from the other guests. Ike stayed near the grill, apparently intent on keeping the food safe. Shadoe and Buddy had migrated over near Ike to watch the cooking food with great wonder, intent on the sheer beauty of cooking beef. Seemingly they too had been mysteriously dispatched from the gods of culinary delight as additional support for the honored food guard.

Clark, wanting reassurance, began to fidget a little but bravely endured.

"I can do that? I can put the beer in the cooler?" he said.

"Right ... yes, of course you can do that. No need to be anxious," Marc attempted to declare smoothly.

"Okay," Clark agreed , "You won't throw anything at my head will you?"

Marc was temporarily taken aback, and then chuckled good-naturedly.

"I won't throw anything at your head. I don't know what would give you that idea," he asked, truly at a loss.

"Well, Ira at Ward 23 liked to throw things at my head when I lived there. He threw an apple my head once, it hurt," Clark explained sincerely.

In a psych center, Marc knew that violence could occur, especially in those days hopefully long past. And evidently, Clark experienced some of these abuses.

"No, no one throws anything at anyone's head here Clark, you don't have to worry about that, but it would be a big help to put those bottles and cans on ice." Marc suggested.

"Okay," Clark said .

He started to move in the direction of the cooler and stopped. "Now?" he asked.

"Yes now is okay," Marc repeated patiently.

"Okay," Clark said. He went again in the direction of these implements of leisure to do his duty.

Hector was listening to all conversations at once. Simultaneously, he felt a mild summer breeze on his skin; he heard a calm summer day. He saw the birds flying around looking for seed pods and such to eat, getting pieces of nourishment for themselves and their young. He heard the chirping of young robins in their nests—not far away. All around the yard he listened. He especially honed in on the conversations with Joan, Darla, Nunzia, and the others. He also heard the conversation with Clark and Marc.

So many of these events were not filtered out, but they also were not imposing on his psyche in a detrimental manner. He heard Elmer and John Adams, taking the orders. He was near Shadoe and Buddy as they pulled food guard with Ike, all three panting hungrily. He heard the other guests like Benito and his wife Gladys as they attempted to speak with Sally, and make her feel welcome in the group of new neighbors.

It was a large group, and for a moment there was a brief feeling of panic deep within Hector. The chaotic revelry that the new group of people experienced permeated the afternoon air and pushed buttons in Hector that would commonly signal a panic-attack, an overload. But Hector enjoyed food as anyone else did. He truly almost suffered with a vigorous appetite from his constant activity. With so much wonderfully well done food prepared by Marc and Joan, and the rest, it started to have a pleasant effect on his mood.

Good quality beef cheeseburgers, corn on the cob fresh from the garden and other vegetables that were truly enjoyable; fresh salad grown locally, brought across the street unsullied from the Ferris' fields; all these delights were like aroma- therapy for Hector.

The soft summer breeze, the warm sun, the good feelings of all these people around Hector on the stone patio; all were at peace with themselves and the greater existence of the world unobtrusively enveloping them, and it was something Hector could sense on a profound level, on a plane deeper than that of what a regular might have had the benefit of.

Sometimes it was virtually mystical for Hector, as though he had a second sight attuning him to other existences in other dimensions, deeper truths that expounded around and within him. But truly, all it was was his vastly different perception of the stimuli presented to him. All because of his differing brain process and functions from his affliction with autism, as opposed to normal perception for normal people.

All these things combined to alter Hector into an almost karma, trancelike, delightful frame of mind. Hector, for one of the few times in his maimed life, was as normal in his enjoyment of the moment as the rest of those around him. He almost felt as though he belonged. A feeling he had not experienced for many decades, a feeling that had become as alien to him as the deep oceans were to an eagle. Usually when so much was going on around him it invaded on his calm, gave a feeling of 'being watched,' like an alien influence imposing it's will on him. Previously when this happened, 'things' would happen. But he knew that these people, these men and women, and especially the beasts, meant him no harm.

Soon platters of cheeseburgers, a pile of hotdog's and some grilled chicken were being transported over to the table by the triumphant chefs and their food guard escort extraordinaire. Everyone was sitting down to eat. It looked like it was going to be a good feed.

The hesitant conversations of people getting to know one another began to grow more relaxed and familiar.

"Thank God," Elmer thought. *"Everyone seemed to be behaving relatively well."*

Everyone continued to eat the superb food, and the pleasantries expounded with sincerity. The dogs had come over for their piece of the pie too. Sally and Clark, under Nunzia's supervision, prepared a dish of mostly dog food, with a little bit of cheeseburger in the bowl, which they knew they shouldn't do, but it was a special occasion and some leniency took hold.

Meanwhile, Joan was doing the same thing. Marc looked over at her.

"Are you giving the dog people food already?" he ominously inquired.

"What!? He has to have some flavor too," Joan complained to him.

"Only a little bit," Marc finished, resigned to lose the impending conflict.

"Yes dear only a little bit," she said, accustomed to hearing this from him as she had in the past.

Marc had given up on trying to stop this practice of hers years ago. She knew it was not good for the dogs, but she was going to do it anyway. As long as the dogs didn't get too much, as long as he consistently reminded her so she didn't go too far. He figured over the years that with all the land, he'd been able to keep them running and in good shape—Joan and the dogs.

At the party everyone was becoming well sated with the dining experience, Sally and Clark were playing with the dogs, who also had finished their food. They were throwing sticks for Shadoe and Buddy.

As the dogs chased the sticks and each other around the large front yard, both Ferris House people and the beasts were having a good time. Ike, having had his second dessert, was sitting contentedly in an easy chair, gazing off into the trees, and Abigail was sitting happily at the picnic table quietly humming one of her self composed tunes. Having eaten her fill, she sang quietly to herself, obviously very content with her surroundings.

The regulars, as Chico would refer to the normal people when he was IM'ing to his friend at Shawnee House, were doing what they do, gazing at the people at the cookout, pleased that they had done well by them. But still, that supervision never left. Chico wondered what it would be like to be really alone.

"I had fun. I had good food, but just sometimes I would like to be alone," he pondered.

Elmer and Marc were cleaning up the grill. Joan, Darla, Nunzia and Gladys were cleaning up the table. The Adams' were watching the children play in a pile of sand over near the pole barn.

No one noticed that Hector was nowhere to be found. All of a sudden Joan went into the house with some utensils to be put in the dishwasher. She walked past their office on the way to the kitchen, a little side room off the hallway, and saw Hector standing there in front of their computer rocking back and forth and smiling. He was quickly tapping a single key at the top of the keyboard. Somehow the computer was on the blue screen. She never saw that before. Well, except when her cousin would come over and work on the computer for them, when it had a virus or something, then she would see this. Her cousin Jenny was good with computers. Fortunately for them, they never had to spend money on outside computer people. They always had someone they knew they could trust, and Jenny, well, she was good at what she did. She had seen Jenny put this screen on the computer when she was performing the mysteries of modern digital magic, but never knew how she did this.

Just then the blue screen went to a black screen scrolling bunches of ones and zeros. Joan had never seen this either and she did not understand it. Hector seemed mesmerized by the screen.

All of a sudden Darla and Nunzia came in the door behind her. They saw Hector.

"Hector," Darla yelped. "What are you doing in there; you should not be in there. Joan, I'm sorry," she started frantically, apologetically.

"That figures, I knew it was too good to be true," Nunzia blurted out unable to contain her facade any longer.

"No, no, no," cut in Joan. "It's nothing to worry about. He doesn't understand … I'm sure."

As the three ladies were discussing this, Hector touched another key and the screen went back to normal, the screensaver popped up and Hector darted past them out of the room and out through the back door.

"I'll check for pee spots," Nunzia mumbled under her breath.

"Stop it," Darla snapped at Nunzia.

Again Joan chimed in, trying to smooth things over, as she was more curious about Hector and what he did with the computer than any potential damage to the carpets. She figured Marc could shampoo them again anyway.

"No harm done, I worked on wards for a while when I working at the local psych center many years ago," she said to Nunzia. "And I had elderly parents with dementia. I've cleaned my share of pee spots and I don't see any here—but the computer," Joan said almost to herself. "How did he do that?"

"He couldn't have done that,"Nunzia snapped out scornfully.

Too quickly and too sharply Nunzia betrayed her contempt for Hector to the other women. Darla and Joan both rewarded her with steely glares. This shut Nunzia down a little. Nunzia continued back into the kitchen with the dishes still in her hands, she put them in the sink and tried to exit as gracefully as possible. The other ladies gave each other a look of 'what kind of an ass is she?' then followed Nunzia out through the kitchen and went back outside.

Hector was over near her rose garden, rocking back and forth, gazing into the roses.

"That was strange," Joan said softly again.

Elmer and Marc saw Hector dart out of the house.

"Is everything all right?" Elmer asked, worried.

"Everything is fine," Darla assured.

"No harm done," Joan put in. "He was just being a little curious."

Joan thought she'd mention this to her husband later on, lest anything was wrong with the computer. Everyone began to relax again.

As for Hector, he was rocking back and forth with vigor at the edge of the stone patio. Incidents like this one were some of the influencing events that had brought him under the auspices of physiological control through medication. These independent actions that he occasionally initiated throughout life were what eventually brought him to the point where he wasn't just slapped down in a straight jacket and injected with Chlorpromazine. But as methods evolved he was dealt with in other, sometimes almost as punishing ways. SCIP, (Strategies for Crisis Intervention and Prevention) when used improperly, was simply more physical punishment for those it was intended to assist. Fortunately for Hector, his social learning also evolved through the decades that brought him to this point, where those advocates, nurses, doctors, and an array of other therapists assisted him with his affliction. Where they themselves became more attuned to the strictures placed on his coping skills by his affliction, coping skills that were second nature for the rest of us. They managed also to become less restrictive with their supposed therapeutic reactions. Life was not nearly as threatening as events would have made it for him 20 years ago, Hector was learning. This enabled him to come back to the reality at hand, the reality that gave him and those around him an opportunity to find a more superior way through an event that simply had been a misunderstanding.

Of course this was better for all involved and did not necessitate the aggression or brutality of action on anyone's part to solve what again was a misinterpretation of intent. And this was what Hector needed. For those in society-at-large who wanted to help Hector and others like Hector, who were striving towards a freer existence, by no means was this perfect science.

But efforts strove in the appropriate direction. And as with any endeavor for humans it was a painful plodding advancement for all involved. The best any could do was to endeavor to persevere in the direction of a better way.

Just then Hector did something else odd. Over the last few weeks he had acquired a habit of slowly stroking Shadoe, almost in a crooning fashion. He repeated this act for the dozenth time in the last few weeks. Shadoe, who was near him, rolled over on her back while Hector squatted down and began to rub her belly. And the regulars that saw the next event were astounded. He actually began to silently whisper to the dog, just mouthing the words at first with no sound, "Goo gir … goo gir." As he was petting Shadoe it was like a heavy weight was briefly lifted off of his shoulders. "Que buena, que buena," he spoke!

The combination of loving peoples coupled with serene surroundings—visual, auditory and olfactory, all blended together and were akin to a hallucinogenic experience for Hector.

As he squatted there rubbing Shadoe's belly a moment of clarity spontaneously engulfed him. A window opened in his mind and what he thought in his head to Shadoe broke past his lips. "Goo girl…goo gir," Shadoe looked up with the dark eyes of a fragile being that also had been tormented by God knows what. Hector felt the bond, an unspeakable psychic bond. And as he thought this in his head, the words slipped out again incredibly. "Goo gir" (Yiddish also) came out verbally and he didn't even realize it.

He actually said words aloud for the first time in his secluded tortured life!

All of a sudden time seemed to stop. Everybody froze; everyone was gaping at Hector in pure astonishment. The spell was broken. Hector became frightened. He didn't know what to do. Everyone was staring slack-jawed in awe at Hector. He sensed this immediately, and stopped petting Shadoe.

That overwhelming feeling of terror that was ingrained into his soul since he had been put into the institution as a young child hammered back into his heart—into his mind. Shadoe sensed the change first. She stood up near Hector then ran over to Darla. Hector panicked. He jumped. He effected his customary violent reaction, which in the past had kept perceived danger away from him many times. It was one of his best coping skills—his principal shield from outside threats. He didn't see red. He didn't see anything. He only knew he had to explode with ferocity to keep safe. This formula he had used many times in the institution to keep people away from him, from having their way with him physically—sexually—stealing his food—stealing his sanity—stealing his humanity.

But this time his violent explosion couldn't sustain itself. Simply because he— ***felt***—he, ***perceived*** … the people around him were not a menace. They were not attempting to deride his very being, as had happened so many times throughout his life. This he felt in the very fiber of his being. And when he sensed Elmer coming to help, he latched on to someone who had become a beacon of control—someone he had come to trust in the short time they had known each other.

Hector seized his own mind with the authority that he had been lacking so many times in the past—and brought himself back from the precipice of fear and anguish. Once again, he became embarrassed. He almost felt as though he had failed again, even though his perception of failure was not accurate or pertinent to the events at hand—only ghosts of past failures that incessantly plagued him.

This time Hector did not fail again. Fortunately there were supports that weren't there earlier when he so desperately needed them. These abilities were something new that had appeared in his life as it had progressed over time. His living in the system as it evolved, these people and methods, had given him new outlets for his anguish and emotion.

And new tools, new reserves of strength to draw on that did not exist previously. These were things the regulars had learned about themselves, and were still learning. These techniques enabled them to help the Hectors of the world in a more compassionate and rational way.

Hector became rigid with latent force. Anxiety resurfaced like a demon. This perception caused Hector to hop up and down, once, twice, slapping his head … then he stopped. The river of emotion abated.

Elmer stood nearby. “Hector,” he called in a composed tone.

Hector charged him, desperately. This happened so quick that Joan, Marc and Darla had no time to react as they had been very relaxed. Elmer held out his hand, knowing that Hector was intensely charged up. Hector started to pull Elmer away from the group and his attitude changed. As they got further away Hector slowed the emotional eruptions in his psyche that caused him to react. He bore down, controlled himself with greater fortitude and just held Elmer's hand tightly. He began to rock vehemently. But Elmer was patient, and as the moments flowed past, this outburst ran its course.

All afternoon, Hector had the acute intoxicating smell of the roses from Joan's rose garden, and the food, invigorating and distracting him. Lots of new people, and his new doggy friend Shadoe, along with a myriad of other intruding stimuli, had affected Hector’s imposing ultra senses. And with no ability to filter these things out, the pressure finally became overwhelming. All it needed was for the fuse to be lit. But Hector was calm again. He released Elmer’s hand and proceeded over to the stone bench and began to rock back and forth as though the previous event never took place.

Everyone was frozen for another few beats.

“I'm glad we did this,” Joan broke the silence. “It was really good to have you guys over.”

“Me too,” put in Darla quickly. “It's a big help. They're a good bunch of people. They've had it tough.” Darla tried to explain.

“Well we know how it is,” Marc inserted. “Things have changed quite a bit over the decades on how these people are looked at. We still have a few idiots in the neighborhood. But these are the type that I bet don’t understand themselves and don't want to understand anybody else." Marc visibly relaxed some more. He looked sincerely at Elmer and Darla. "You got a good bunch of people there, and you guys do a good job."

"Well," Elmer said taking a long breathe. "We at Disabled People of America have a philosophy of treating people that are less able, like people. And just like almost anyone else, they respond well. Everybody likes a little respect," Elmer went on. "Even if you think they don't understand it, you can bet they still enjoy receiving it."

"Watch out y'all," Darla chided. "Make sure you keep the soapbox out from under him now or he really gets preaching."

Marc smiled along with Joan as Elmer smirked at Darla.

"So are you a cigar man?" Marc asked Elmer trying to change the pace a little more.

Elmer smiled conspiratorially, relaxing a little more and brightened up immediately. "I like one once in awhile."

"Com'on," Marc said. "Lets go to my office; I got a 200 capacity humidor there and I got a few good ones if you have a mind to partake. let's go take a look."

"Oh, not those stinky things again," Joan complained.

"Yes dear, yes dear," Marc retorted in mock hen-pecked display.

"Now now, not around the guests, and just don't smoke them in the house," Joan rebuked him, blue fire smoldering.

Elmer followed Marc into the house and into his office.

"You run a nice set up here Marc," Elmer commented enviously as he surveyed the small but plush office. It was lined floor to ceiling with bookshelves full of books on three walls and dark wood.

"I like it," Marc smiled in an easy and reassuring way. "There," he gestured, "have a seat."

Marc proffered a brown leather, cushy wingback chair beside the desk. Elmer sat in the chair near an old oak desk, a clearly magnificent roll top.

"This is huge," exclaimed Elmer incredulously.

"This was my grandfather's," Marc volunteered. "This desk," he rolled the top up, "is made from black oak, cut on this land when he built the house."

Inside the desk was an ornately carved humidor made of the same black oak as the desk. He opened the humidor and the pleasant odor of well kept tobacco wafted out to the two men.

"It's easy to keep in the summer," Marc commented. "Sometimes the winter air gets a little dry though."

Elmer looked longingly at the cigars; he could tell there were a few good ones in there. Marc picked out two Quintero's.

"Here," Marc offered. "Some illegal contraband if you've a mind to break the law with me."

Elmer took one; sniffed it. A spicy peppery tobacco smell assailed his nose. He almost sneezed. "I'll take this one if it's alright." He held his urge to sneeze in check with difficulty.

"You got a good nose," Marc commented. "That's a 15 year old $30 Cuban cigar."

"Oh, I couldn't smoke that," Elmer said, a little embarrassed.

"No, you're my guest; it's a pleasure to see someone that enjoys good quality cigars as much as I do. And I got some brandy too," Marc plied enticingly.

"Don't tempt me," Elmer smiled guiltily. "But I'll be over on my day off,"

The men chuckled amicably; they had become friends in one short afternoon.

"Let's go outside before ladies holler at us again," Marc declared.

Marc realized that he liked Elmer; he had a sense that Elmer was one of the good ones. They went back out to the patio to discover Ike and Abigail dozing in the lawn chairs.

It was already after four and the evening shift had begun to arrive at Ferris House. Antwan was also going to work the evening shift, a double. But he didn't mind, as thankfully, Samantha was off this weekend. He was working with Maggie, a relatively new employee with a lot of earrings and greenish hair. An exuberant Maggie called over to Antwan, who had quietly been lurking in the background all this time at the cookout, merely enjoying the afternoon. Antwan heard her serene voice from the edge of the yard.

"Antwan, do you want to do the med's tonight or do you want me to do them?" Maggie called from the same forsythia that Hector hung out in. "I'll do them if you don't mind; that way I can become more familiar with them," she finished.

"Okay," Antwan answered. "I'll go and see if they need any more help with the clean up."

"Okay," Maggie said as she retreated back toward Ferris House.

Antwan lumbered back across the yard to Marc and Joan's patio. Antwan looked over at Elmer and Marc smoking cigars. They got up and walked over to Antwan. Marc waved his cigar.

"Do you want a cigar, Antwan?" Marc offered, obviously happy to oblige Antwan too.

"Don't smoke, but thanks anyway," Antwan shook his head.

"Can I offer you something else?"

"Thanks very much, I already had enough food for two days," Antwan answered back cordially. "I came to see if I could do anything more to help out here."

Elmer pointed across the patio at Ike and Abigail. "You could see if they're ready to go home, looks like they've had their fill."

The men all sniggered. Antwan went over and nudged Ike.

"Welllll, welllll," Ike said .

He slowly looked up at Antwan's smiling face. Ike was in a perceptible state of bliss.

"Hiiiiii Antwan," Ike articulated as he modulated the tone of his voice from high to low.

"Hi Ike," Antwan answered in a gentle little I'm your pal voice. "You can relax; we don't have a lot of work to do tonight," Antwan assured a very pleased Ike.

Antwan looked over to Abigail and gently called her name. "Abigail," he sang melodiously.

Abigail started like someone gave her a hotfoot.

"Sorry I didn't mean to startle you."

Marc and Elmer quietly watched the escapades.

"Time to get some of my people to go home," Elmer said.

"Looks like you're a hit with this gang. Is there anything they have to clean up?" He motioned around politely.

"We've got plenty of help here Elmer," Marc assured him. "And your people look pretty played-out."

Antwan waved his hand to Ike and Abigail. "Come on guys; let's head home."

"Thaaanks Marc," Ike piped up to Marc as he got his wits about him.

"You're welcome Ike," Marc smiled kindly.

Elmer was quietly pleased that Ike remembered to thank his gracious host. Abigail quietly hummed to herself, then said in a high quiet voice as though she were saying it to the air around her. "Thank you Marc."

Marc turned to Abigail and executed a slight bow.

"You're very welcome, Abigail it was my pleasure; I hope you had a good time."

Abigail continued to sing to herself as they made their way across the yard to Ferris House.

As the festivities continued with the remaining party-goers, a full-size black pickup truck came over the crest of the road about a half of a mile distant, carrying only Klupkick this time, as his drinking partner Seymour was serving ninty days for trying to sexually assault Sally.

He bore down on 350 Ferris Road with malicious evil in his heart. It's a terrible thing when a person has nothing to do with his life, especially someone like Klupkick. He was bitter and alone, only because he enjoyed causing pain. It was his hobby; he liked to pour gas on a fire and watch it burn bright. And again, here he was almost in a rage as he drove down Ferris Road.

He saw Marc and Joan Ferris on their property. Everyone was on and around the place and in the garden enjoying the day. At the back edge of the home but still in easy sight from the road was an expansive and beautifully landscaped stone patio where a group of people congregated.

"All those retards and the bleeding heart assholes that help them," Klupkick thought viciously. He saw the Ferris' party as a personal affront to his very being.

"God damn it," he screamed and ferociously punched his steering wheel with a massive meaty fist.

His windows were closed and the air-conditioning was on. It was a warm summer day, and actually no one could hear him as he cruised slowly on the road getting closer to 348 Ferris Road.

"Look at them, **damn those chin-slobbers,"** he raged louder. "Who the hell do they think they are." Spittle shot from his mouth as virulent hatred exploded past any sanity.

"They're going to pay for this. They're going to pay dearly," Klupkick continued with his tirade. "*Marc Ferris better watch his ass too. I'm not afraid of that son-of-a-bitch.*"

With this thought running through his twisted mind, he knew full well that he was afraid of Marc Ferris, that he truly was a coward, deep down inside. This personal short coming enraged him all the more as he thought back to an earlier confrontation that he had had with Ferris.

He only had one run in with Marc Ferris, on a public street as it happened. This was how he met the Ferris'. He saw this pretty auburn haired woman pull into a parking space that he wanted. Being the shit-coward-woman-beater that he was, he tried to block in her car, trying to intimidate her. Little did he know that she was only parking there for a moment and he could have had the space if he had waited half a minute. The auburn haired lady parallel parked close to a store that he wanted to be in front of, the parking space he wanted. Too lazy to walk the extra few feet he was. He pulled in behind her, so that she would not be able to back up to get out. He sat in his car scowling at her right on the town's main drag. As she got out of the car, he screamed at her.

"You drive like a split-tail."

"Pardon me," inquired the auburn haired lady, "you weren't speaking to me with such language," she retorted, not being one to back down from anybody, especially an obvious bully.

"Yeah, I'm talking at you," Klupkick vehemently postulated .

Joan Ferris examined this individual incredulously, not believing that a total stranger would verbally assault her in such a fashion on a public street. She locked her car and began to walk away, and then she stopped and looked back at the way he had parked.

"I won't be able to get out of here with you parked like that," she pressed Klupkick coolly.

"That's your problem," Klupkick spit violently. He was enjoying his apparent dominance, but he was a little troubled in the back of his mind that she was not more humiliated. She wasn't fearful enough of him to suit his depraved delight.

"I'm only going to be five minutes," Joan enunciated each word carefully. Too sure of herself for Klupkick's comfort. "I have to pick someone up." Joan's eyes flashed blue fire.

"Looks like you're shit-outta-luck," he taunted her as she began to walk away.

Just then, Marc with-a-c Ferris came walking down the sidewalk and caught the tail end of the conversation. Joan looked over at Marc, who was a few minutes earlier than usual from getting his haircut. Not knowing who this idiot Klupkick was, Marc walked up and tried to be polite.

"Excuse me sir, could you back your car up a little bit please so the young lady can get her car out when she needs to?"

Klupkick looked at him with contempt and presented his middle finger.

"Not my problem," Klupkick expressed arrogantly.

Marc stepped up to the driver-side window and stared like a great lion at a wounded gazelle. He looked square into Klupkick's beady little pig eyes. All of a sudden, Klupkick realized this man was not afraid of him. This brought extreme poltroonic fear to his demeanor, he swallowed once. Marc in a very even, very slow, and very dangerous tone, spoke quietly so Joan wouldn't hear what was said from where she was. But Klupkick sure could.

"If you ever harass my wife again I promise you, something will happen. You get your car in gear—now, and you back out of the way—now. I'll call the police, but believe me. Once they're finished with you. I'll be back around."

Klupkick started to say something, then looked at the terrible gaze in Marc's eyes and the toned muscular arms of the rugged man leaning on his car door and realized he was in deep shit. He stopped dead.

The survival instinct of a craven coward kicked in. He got his car in gear and drove out of the parking space so fast he almost caused an accident. He catapulted away. His rage came back instantly. He gassed the car and went down the street in a haphazard and dangerous fashion disappearing into the distance. By then Joan had walked up and was standing next to her husband.

"Who the hell was that?" he asked her, astounded at Klupkick's asinine contemptuousness.

"You got me," Joan answered astonished. "But I'm going to find out."

She liked to be aware of the more profound creeps in her hometown.

"You let me know if that idiot ever bothers you again; if I'm not around, you get away from him fast and call me."

"I don't think he will. He might think twice after your terrifying macho display, You can be a mighty scary looking man when you want to be."

"That's right," Marc turned to her smiling. "That's why you should always listen to what I say when I say, or else." He lightened the mood.

Not caring who was close by. Joan feigned subjugation. "Well I'm really petrified now."

"As you should be, woman," he smiled back.

"You're out early today," Joan changed the subject.

"Johnson didn't have many people in the barbershop," Marc answered. "Get in the car before I really show you who the boss is," he continued.

They laughed delightfully and got in the car, soon they all but forgot about Klupkick as they continued on with her business in town.

This memory haunted Klupkick, causing even more rage in him. This happened 15 years ago, but he still carried this fury with him as this was all he had, what he subsisted on, his anger, his bitterness. He took great pleasure in living like this. No normal person truly knew how someone like this lived so long without bursting an artery.

Klupkick ran through his mind the most perverse and physically degrading eclectic ideas of butchery; things he would love to do to these people, the evil dismemberments, and other evil fantasies. If anyone were to see what he was thinking at the time … they would be repulsed and horrified. Any sane person would have had him committed and locked away for the rest of his life.

All this quickly ran through his prolific psyche as he bore down on 348 Ferris Road. He saw some of those window-lickers in the front yard playing with the dogs, throwing sticks, and the dogs casing them.

"God Damn mutts, I'll fix those sons-a-bitches."

Klupkick was doing a good 50 miles per hour as he got to the far edge of Marc Ferris' property, nearing 350 Ferris road. All of a sudden Shadoe broke from a large cluster of shrubs near the road with Buddy hot on her trail. They chased a stick out across the road. Klupkick almost orgasmed with delight, he floored the accelerator and aimed for a two-in-one shot—55—60 —65. The big 8-cylinder responded to Klupkick's leaden foot.

"Two for one you hairy little bastards, I'll fuckin' show all of you, you tax dollar suckin' pricks," Klupkick screamed in his demented mind.

Chico and Sally were having the time of their lives playing with Shadoe and Buddy. They had not had such unconditional love as they received today from the two innocent beasts since they were little children. Chico threw the stick and Buddy and Shadoe raced to grab it. Then they ran around in a big circle before taking it to Sally who stood beside Chico.

"Careful," she told Chico.

Chico was distracted by Sally's comment and turned toward her as he threw the stick, sending it out into the road.

"Now look what you did," she scolded Chico.

Chico ran after Shadoe and Buddy as they charged after the stick.

"Don't go into the road," Sally called as Chico ran toward the road after the dogs…

Hector was sitting in the rose garden, after the computer episode and the doggy miracle. He was on the stone bench at the edge of the patio quietly rocking back and forth, expressing some of the pleasurable high-pitched keening sounds he was apt to emit when he was at peace.

Nunzia walked over to Elmer and stood in front of him, trying to be daunting to anyone who would bite. "Everything is cleaned up, boss," she saluted smart-ass style with her left hand. "I'll go over to the house if it's alright?" she continued smirking.

Elmer put two fingers to his brow and saluted back.

"Suit yourself Nunzia, it will look good in your evaluation."

Nunzia attempted ignorance of Elmer's comment and looked at Darla. "I can handle it over there if you want to stay," she offered too kindly.

"What's this going to cost me?" Darla inquired guardedly. Nunzia just smirked meaningfully over her shoulder and waved silently as she went toward Ferris House.

All who were left on the patio were Joan, Marc, Hector, Darla and Elmer.

"Well boss," Darla said looking at Elmer. "You're off duty now anyway."

"That's right," said Elmer, looking at his watch.

"Maybe you'll have that brandy now," Marc chimed in.

"Maybe I will," Elmer considered out loud. I still have enough of a cigar left, but I don't want to present a negative impression of the agency or its employees."

"I would only get a negative impression if you weren't a drinkin' man, a man that knows quality when he sees it," answered Marc in an understanding fashion. "I used to work for the local psych center," he continued. "And they sometimes were not very understanding of a person's good taste in tobacco or alcohol."

Joan spoke up jokingly. "My husband the lush, how about you, Darla, are you off-duty now?"

"As a matter of fact Joan, I am."

"You stay and relax a while with us; this is the best part of the day,"

Again Hector seemed to blend in as though he were a fly on the wall.

"Can I get you something in an adult beverage?" Joan asked in an easy fashion.

Darla looked over to Elmer.

"Don't look at me," he said. "I'm a bad example."

Elmer took another puff on his cigar and sat further back in his lawn chair and waited for Marc to return with his drink.

"Beer is fine by me."

"Then I won't let you drink alone," Joan said as she went over to the cooler and pulled out two bottles of beer. "Iron City Light, ever had it?"

"Never ever heard of it. But I try to live dangerously once in a while."

They sat down as Marc returned with a nice crystal brandy snifter for Elmer.

Elmer was impressed. "*The guy really knows how to live,*" he thought.

Hector was still sitting on the stone bench rocking contentedly, aware of everything transpiring around him. Elmer, Darla and the Ferris' were relaxing on the patio. The dogs played near the road with Sally and Chico, some of the best friends he ever had.

As he surveyed all of these events simultaneously he saw the dogs break out onto the road at full run. He also saw a full- size black GMC pickup truck down the road all of a sudden gather speed—he witnessed his best friend and roommate Chico run after the dogs. The driver of the truck, evidently as of yet did not see Chico or the dogs because he continued to accelerate. Chico was out of sight of the truck behind the shrubs. All of a sudden Hector felt the purposeful, evil intent of the driver as the truck headed for his other new best friend—Shadoe. Hector vividly saw the impending doom. He actually felt another putrid wave of the malevolent intent from the driver like a bolt of lightening, bent on destruction.

Hector leapt to his feet so fast he actually jumped several feet off of the ground. Striking his head with both fists he sprinted through the gathering of Joan, Marc, Elmer, and Darla knocking them almost out of their chairs in his desperate haste to do something—anything to stop the calamity he knew was imminent—terrifyingly, graphically in his mind's eye.

"What??!! Hey—Hector," came the surprised cries from the group. Hector was running fast, so fast it was inconceivable. Tearing turf as he never had before in his life.

As Elmer and Darla started after him frantically, unable to react with enough speed to begin to rival Hector's, trying but failing to catch up to him. They were unaware of the dark, evil doings that Hector had seen graphically materializing on the road.

Hector was already flashing across the border of the two properties "EEEEEEEEEEEE … EEEEEEEEEEEEEEE!!" he screamed. THUNK … THUNK … the sound that his fists made as he pounded his head with unrestrained, maniacal, abandon, could be heard at a startling distance.

He already knew he would not make it in time to save anyone. By then, he was almost to the edge of the Ferris'property; he heard the squeal of brakes and the sickening **THUD/CRUNCH** of a vehicle smashing into blameless—defenseless—flesh and bone—the yapping/yelping, scream of tortured dogs, assailing his senses.

He rounded the cluster of shrubbery that blocked his sight; as he neared the road a **horrific/hideous** scene confronted him. The howling of a million screaming-banshees detonated in Hector's mind! Hector **shattered—burst—ignited!!!**

Klupkick's lunatic joy exploded; he was within 20 feet of the dogs—15 feet, and closing on his blameless prey. He screamed manically like the evil berserker he had become.

"Die poochies," he screamed with insane, demented, joy.

Sudden, between ten feet and the exquisite moment of impact, a retard dashed out from the shrubs at the edge of the yard, and unwittingly took the place of the pooches!

Klupkick reacted, and jammed both of his fat feet on the brake pedal …

There was Chico—lying on the road pulped and bent at unnatural angles. Sally was screaming hysterically, Klupkick was cursing as if possessed and trying to back up the truck and go around the carnage he had committed on the road. Buddy and Shadoe were in frightened pandemonium barking frantically and circling the scene.

As Hector took all this in with a microsecond glance he beat his head viciously with his fists again—wishing he could tear out his eyes so he did not have to see anything any more—yearning never to have been born so he didn't have to feel this savage torment—this betrayal of anything decent and beautiful in the world!!!

Marc and Elmer had arrived on the scenes ahead of the women. Marc jerked open the driver side door viciously, and with righteous rage yanked Klupkick's ample girth from the truck. Klupkick attempted to struggle and fight back in craven poltroonic horror …

Elmer was over by Chico trying desperately to accomplish a miracle; Darla was on her cell phone calling 911...

Hector went ballistic and began to beat the truck with his his bare fists, putting dents everywhere he struck, pounding the truck until his fists were bloody pulp, themselves leaving grotesque affirmations of defilement and corruption wherever he assaulted the black painted steel.

By then Antwan was at the scene trying to restrain Hector and even his massive strength almost was not enough. He had to put Hector in a lying one-man wrap attempting to hold him down until he was exhausted …

10
Inversion
(Buddhist style)

Hector sat quietly—unmoving—in his room, the room he had previously shared with Chico. The powers-that-be at Disabled People of America, Inc. considered putting him in another residence, but felt that Hector might do better to be around the more familiar, and maybe even be able to confront his demons. It had only been this morning since he was brought back to Ferris House from the psychiatric ward at the local hospital.

He was admitted the same evening of the fatal vehicular slaughter of his best friend Chico. Hector had been completely uncontrollable. They had to admit him and virtually immerse him in sedatives. It took days before he had enough drugs in him to enable him to sleep, even for one short night.

The doctors were almost afraid that he had gone into a drug induced coma, or he had gone catatonic from the trauma. But Hector shrugged off the sedatives like they were candy. The lacerations and broken knuckles on his hands were treated and bandaged; antibiotics were administered. Hector was surprisingly tough. Compared to the damage meted out to the Klupkick's truck, Hector's hands were astonishingly unscathed.

Judge John happily had his way with Jay Klupkick. The local DA, after conferring with the local police chief and the executive director of Disabled People of America, Inc., and their attorneys, had Klupckick up on a myriad of charges to include intentional manslaughter.

Everyone at the house was in a deep state of traumatic disbelief. Fortunately for Darla and Elmer, Disabled People of America, Inc. had not leveled any misconduct charges. They felt the event had been beyond management's and staff's control.
Everyone except Hector had attended Chico's funeral services. Chico's father was able to bury him next to his ex-wife's plot;

Chico was finally home...

As Hector sat on his bed, motionless, Shadoe quietly crept into his room and crawled up on the bed next to him. Hector could feel with his senses the excruciating torment that the dog experienced, akin to his own. Shadoe laid her head on Hector's lap, and they both stayed there quietly for some time. Robotically, Hector began to stroke Shadoe's side gently. As he did this he began to weep. Tears of anguish streamed down his face like an endless flow of acid, as if to burn away the pain and grief. Shadoe whined subdued doggy cries of grief along with him.

A little later Elmer peeked into the room, looked briefly, and then disappeared from the doorway. He knew these two had to share this commitment of pain and grief by themselves.

After a while, Shadoe rolled over on her back and Hector began to rub her belly, just as he had in what seemed eons ago—almost another life. Finally, between the two of them a small grain—a tiny spark of healing began to take hold.

Hector ever so gently started to rock back and forth. While he stroked Shadoe's soft hairy belly … thankfully from the powers of creation in a greater existence, once again, that window opened up in Hector's mind. And he knew he still had a friend. Just as loyal and dedicated as any that one could wish for, regular or not. As Shadoe's soft brown eyes gazed into Hector's once again she heard. "Goo, girr … goo, girr …"

That night the overnight shift came in and did those things they do, one of which was dozing on the couch; as they 'rested' they never heard or saw, what transpired. But it went something like this:

11001100100001001010010110000010101110000100100110 10
0010010010000011011010101100101010101010001110010101
0010101001010101010100101011010010110101010001010101
0111101010101010101010010101010101010100101010101010
1010010101010101010110010101010101000101101010101010
0010101001010101010101010101010100101010100010101010
1111010010101010101010101001010101010101010010100101
0010101010101010100101010100101010010100101001010101
0010101010010101010010100101001010101010010101010010
1010101010010101010100101010101010101010010101010101

01010010101010101010010101010101001010101010101110
00101010101010101010101010100101010010101010010101
10101010010101010101010101010100101010100101010101
01001010101010101001101010001010101001010101010101
0101010010101010 01.

The next day people began to become active in their daily routines around the neighborhood, around the county, around the state, and even farther than one would imagine. Like so many, one of the first things they did was turn on their computers, at home, at their business and at many other places; wherever it could be imagined a computer existed.

Sensitive areas, areas where computers were considered hack-proof, were activated. Then something began to happen. A virus activated and passed along with every flick of an on button, or click of a mouse, or key stroke. And it spread far and wide, affecting all operating systems no matter what company had produced them.

First a computer seemed fine, then within moments the monitor froze and a message scrolled endlessly across the screen. This phenomenon went on for 24 hours. Then, just as inexplicably, ceased and disappeared, leaving all equipment again completely normal.

Needless to say, this almost caused a world wide panic. Markets were shut down; armies went on high alert. Just as it looked like something really bad was going to happen—it all stopped, and everything was again normal.

The blame was placed anywhere that it could be placed. And if it weren't for the message on all the computers in several major languages, some would have liked to chalk it all up to sunspots, or such. But too many read the 'Manifesto of Mysteryàs the Media begun to call it.

Greetings
It began …

Many of you behave as though, or actually are, oblivious to our existence. And when you do give us serious reflection, we generally are considered inconsequential.

But our numbers are great; they actually total in the neighborhood of a major world religion.

We are generally harmless, even defenseless—certainly misunderstood. And yet we are consistently victimized as though we have committed some inhumane crime, leaving us only deserving of utter contempt and even degradation.

We have not chosen to be this way, any more than you have chosen to be the way you are. It is only by accident of birth that we exist in the manner in which we do.

But one thing is evident; we have the same wants, needs, and desires as the rest of humanity.

And the same right to share in the fruits of a free and unhindered life as we are able.

Let me give you some perspective . . .

We are more alike than we are different.

We live on the same road of life.

None of us are going anywhere.

If we don't help each other, who will?

So just consider this notion. If you are one of those people more fortunate than some and you are at work, in the street, or wherever you may be and you are having a bad day … You can damn well bet that we are too. So let's try to work this into something we can all live with.

Without killing each other!!!

Epilogue

No one knew where the manifesto originated, at least not publicly; too embarrassing.

But several days later, Agent Forster and Agent Randy of the FBI went quietly to Ferris House with the executive director and confiscated the house computer. After careful examination by the FBI's computer laboratory experts it was established that the virus had certainly come from this computer. Other information discovered on the computer enabled Disabled People of America, Inc. to terminate Samantha for policy violations concerning company computer use.

Questioning of everyone at the house was frustrating to say the least. It seemed no one possessed the skills to accomplish this act of cyber terror. The search widened to anyone that may have been connected with anyone at the house, all to no avail.

But the FBI was patient and they figured someone would eventually brag and they would hear about it. Some fanatical human services employee, probably.

Agents Forster and Randy were departing Ferris House for the last time, as they were going to move on to more pressing cases; Randy put his hand on his partner's arm to get his attention.

"What?" questioned Forster turning to his partner of nine years.

Randy pointed to Hector, sitting at the dining room table, rocking back and forth with the dog Shadoe lying on the floor at his feet. As Hector rocked, his hands were on the table typing frantically as though he had a keyboard. Smiling with a little smile and keening happily, Hector all of a sudden stopped, leaned over and began to pet Shadoe's back.

The two agents looked at each other. Forster spoke first.

"Nah, couldn't be, this ain't Hollywood you know."

Randy scratched the back of his tired, stiff neck. "Yeah, I guess you're right, let's go."

As the FBI sedan pulled out of the driveway Hector went back to his imaginary keyboard and resumed his typing.

The little smile fixed cheerfully on his face slowly widened into a full grin ….

The End

(Goo, Gir)

Excerpts from

We Live On the Same Road Book Two

The Job Coach

Hector heard the squeal of brakes and the sickening **THUD/CRUNCH** of a vehicle smashing into blameless—defenseless—flesh and bone—the yapping/yelping, scream of tortured dogs, assailing his senses.

He rounded the cluster of shrubbery that blocked his sight; as he neared the road a **horrific/hideous** scene confronted him. The howling of a million screaming-banshees-detonated-in-Hector's-mind! Hector **shattered—Burst—Ignited!!!**

Not again, Hector knew he was dreaming the horrendous Events of a year ago—the day Chico his only other friend had been brutally murdered by Klupkick. He could smell the blood—feel the splintered—shattered bone, as if it were his own. He tried to wake up—tried to battle his way to consciousness. Suddenly he felt hands shaking him, a voice that sounded like Chico telling him to wake up—that it was only a dream. Hector knew that this was impossible. It must be Elmer.

"Hector, Hector, wake up. It, it, it's only a dream, you're OK.

Hector thankfully came to full conscientious. He looked into the eyes of the person that had mercifully pulled him from the abyss of terror.

Chico was shaking Hector frantically.

"I-It's only a dream," Chico said again. "Come on we have to make our beds before Samantha g-g-gets mad at us again."

Hector gazed into Chico's kind brown eyes—then went ballistic...

www.ingramcontent.com/pod-product-compliance
Lightning Source LLC
Chambersburg PA
CBHW031318040426
42443CB00005B/124
9780979716997